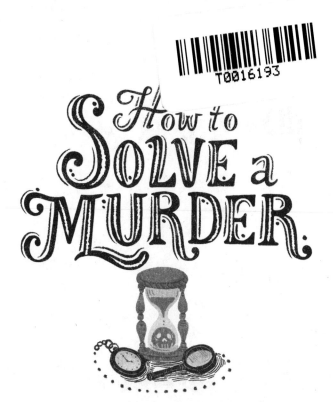

How to Solve a Murder

70 ONE-MINUTE DETECT-O-GRAM MYSTERIES to DECIPHER & DECODE

H. A. RIPLEY

CASTLE POINT BOOKS
NEW YORK

Contents

Crack, the Detect-o-grams

In this book of mysteries—dusted off from 1932 and presented to you in their purest forms with but little adjustment for time and language—you will discover Mr. H. A. Ripley's excellently thought-out detect-o-grams—puzzles to detect and decode like an at-home criminologist who is not bogged down by the pressures of law enforcement and instead retains a bird's eye as crystal clear as an eagle's. These mysteries are not unlike what crime solvers of the day would have encountered; the points of evidence are cleverly assembled and the nuances of incrimination are very subtly shaded. Written in less than two hundred and sixty words, these little stories can be read in a minute.

The following 70 detect-o-grams are not just from any set of files. They have been collected from one Professor Fordney's casebook. You will read more about the Professor and his methods very soon through an old recorded conversation, but what you should know about his philosophy of criminology is that crime is simple. Most criminals are caught not by any superhuman qualities of the detective, but by the criminal's own ignorance, stupidity, or carelessness.

A word of advice: when immersing yourself in the cases presented, take the time to think not as a detective would, but as the criminal in the case. The correct solution will reveal itself to you. In order to understand a mystery—or even how to rehabilitate a criminal once they are in confinement—it is necessary to understand the criminal's personal problems. To accomplish this, a detective must think as the criminal thinks, uncover the reasons the criminal uses to continue their antisocial activities, and from there make use of these findings to assist the criminal toward rehabilitation. Here, you must merely think as the criminal to crack the case.

In these cases, every fact, every clue necessary to the solution is given. The answer is in the story itself. As with all cold cases, you must put yourself in the shoes of someone of the era. Travel back to the late 1920s when Professor Fordney likely penned his case files to make the most of the clues given. Milk was delivered to doorsteps, watches had to be wound, and moonshine was the drink of choice. Each problem has only one possible solution. Here is your chance to work on an even playing field with the Professor, to match your wits with his and the criminal's. You know as much as the Professor does. Now you have an opportunity to prove just how good a detective you are and what poor detectives your friends are. Once finished with your detective work, check your methods by referring to the solutions pages at the back of the book to see if you have what it takes to be a true detective.

Party Game Version

You can solve these mysteries in your spare time for pure enjoyment, or you can make it a game for a party of any size.

It can be played in either of two ways. The first method puts the emphasis on the powers of reasoning and analysis, while the second places a premium on an accurate memory.

1. Select one or more of the minute mysteries that particularly appeal to you. Make as many copies of each as there are guests at the party. Then pass the copies around and allow three minutes, say, for your guests to study them. At the end of this time, each person must hand you a written solution, giving the line of reasoning that was used. Compare these with the solutions at the back of the book. The person who solves the most cases is the winner.

2. Instead of making copies of each story, read it aloud, slowly and carefully. If any of the listeners so desire, it may be read a second time. But after this, no questions may be asked. After the agreed-upon period of time has elapsed, each guest writes out their solution and hands it to you for comparison with the book.

Now that you have all of the tools you need to become a detect-o-gram-solving sleuth, proceed to learn more about your counterpart and criminologist mentor, Professor Fordney. We hope you enjoy the opportunity to use your wits for cracking codes, uncovering lies, and learning *How to Solve a Murder*.

Let Professor Fordney, Super Sleuth, Be Your Guide

Here's all you need to know about the detective who will see you through these cases. Read the descriptions of Professor Fordney from his boss, Chief Inspector Kelley, to get a sense of your partner.

Chief Inspector Kelley, that grizzled veteran of the Detective Bureau, was talking to his nephew, Jim Barry, who had indicated a desire to enter the uncrowded field of criminology. "The average policeman," he said, "looks upon the average criminologist in much the same way as anyone would look negatively upon an amateur. Generally speaking, that attitude is justified.

"In thirty years of police work, however, I have met no one in detective circles, in or out of the force, who so effectively combines theoretical knowledge with practical application as Professor Fordney.

"Even though he's a man of definite scientific achievement and recognition, he still appreciates that the simple fundamentals of crime detection are the key to solving ninety per cent of all criminal cases. While he has used scientific detection to unravel some amazing and extremely baffling crimes that otherwise would have gone unsolved, he puts his greatest reliance on basic crime-solving principles.

"His major theory is that most crimes are simple; that their solution calls only for the exercise of ordinary talents developed to an extraordinary degree; that the stupidity of the average criminal himself, and not the brilliance of the detective, is responsible for his detection. The Professor is known among psychologists as having an authoritative insight into the criminal mind. His greatest interest is his class in criminology at the University. He still finds time, however, to actively assist the police across the country, who frequently consult him on cases they find unusually puzzling.

"There are instances also in which his part has been that of a bystander, where a modest word of suggestion has frequently solved cases before they were brought to the attention of the police. If the Professor is convinced you have the natural qualifications, Jim, and a real inclination for work, I can get you into his class. He will take not only a personal, but a fatherly, interest in you, as in the rest of his students. You will receive the finest possible training given by a man of broad understanding and great human sympathies. Out of his vast experience and knowledge, gained in studying crime in all parts of the world, he will develop in you those qualities essential to success in this field.

"You will find him a friendly, healthy, kindly man of fifty, with a waistline of forty. There is nothing subtle in his face or manner. A characterful nose rises above a strong and determined mouth, adorned by a blond mustache. A pair of keen but smiling blue eyes complete a commonplace face. Although he refuses to admit it, his rapidly thinning hair causes him great concern.

A bit vain, the old codger, but don't tell him I told you so," laughed the Inspector.

"Scrupulously dressed, he looks like an amiable and highly successful business executive. He's a mixer and thoroughly enjoys the good things of life. He views the passing parade with a keen sense of humor, few illusions, and a genuine interest in his fellow man. Detests hypocrisy; would rather see ten guilty men acquitted than one innocent man condemned. Recognizes his own fallibility, but knows his own worth and does not suffer from that abominable social vice, false modesty.

"You might be interested in knowing his only hobby is that of designing, making, and repairing toys for children. He's known to hundreds of them as the Toy Man. Though a bachelor, he looks with favor on the ladies, enjoys their company, and is thoroughly sociable. It's a pleasure and an education to know him. More than once he's helped your old uncle and absolutely refused the credit that was his," concluded Inspector Kelley.

You now have everything you need to solve the following 70 detect-o-grams. Good luck.

A Crack Shot

Professor Fordney was hunting in the Rockies when he heard of a tragedy at one of the camps. Thinking he might be of some help, he went over. Butler, the victim's friend, described the accident.

"When Marshall hadn't returned to camp at nine o'clock last night, I was a bit worried because he didn't know these mountains. There wasn't a star out and it was dark and moonless, so I decided to look around for him. We're five miles from anyone, you know.

"I put more wood on the fire and then set out to look for him. After searching for an hour, I was coming up the slope of a ravine when I saw a pair of eyes shining out at me in the dark. I called out twice to no response, so I fired, thinking it was a mountain lion. I then struck a match, and imagine my horror when I reached the spot and saw I had nearly blown the head off Marshall. A terrible experience!

"I carried his body back to camp and then walked to the nearest house to report the accident."

"How far from camp did you find Marshall?" asked Professor Fordney.

"About a quarter of a mile."

"I see your right hand is bandaged. How do you manage to shoot with it?"

"Oh, I use either hand."

"Mind if I look at the gun?"

"Not at all," said Butler, handing it over.

"Hm, European make. Had it long?"

"No, it's rather new."

"So why did you deliberately murder Marshall?" demanded Fordney abruptly. "Because that's what you did."

○ ○ ○

How did the Professor know Butler had murdered his friend?

(solution on page 152)

On the Scent

"I couldn't wait to be announced," said George Collins, Florida's leading prohibition agent and a man of great wit. He stepped into the Professor's office.

"How long are you going to be in New York?" asked Fordney as he shook his friend's hand.

"I'm due back in Miami now," replied Collins, "but I wanted to congratulate you on your success in the Hicks murder case. I wish interesting things like that would happen in my game. However, I did have an amusing experience last December.

"Sneaky Joe, a stool-pigeon, tipped me off to a huge alcohol still he said was working about forty miles from Headquarters. A narrow road through dense woods led to the spot. Arriving there, I found an old dilapidated shanty screened by trees. As I entered the woods, I smelled alcohol. Sneaky Joe was right, after all, I thought, as I drove up to the shanty.

"I got out and peered cautiously around, but the place seemed deserted. After opening the door and entering the house, however, I knew liquor was not being made there. I searched the woods, but found nothing. As I was driving back along the road at a good rate, I discovered the alcohol I smelled was coming from my own radiator! Imagine my chagrin!"

The Professor laughed heartily and said to his friend, "Stay over for my birthday party tonight, the ladies would love to hear that gag of yours."

○ ○ ○

What did the Professor find preposterous in Collins's story?

(solution on page 152)

Fatal Error

"Crowley was an eccentric and taciturn old fellow, but I liked him," remarked Fordney. "When he was found dead last December, I took a personal interest in the case. Harold Bronson, his last known visitor, had this to say of his visit:

"'After leaving word at my hotel where I might be reached if wanted, I arrived at Crowley's suburban estate shortly after five o'clock. I found him seated in the dusk at the end of his library table. Courteously enough for him, he waved me into a chair at the other end and invited me to dine with him at eight o'clock. Reaching for my cigarettes, I remembered that Crowley did not permit smoking.

"'His principal contributions to our discussion were his usual nods of approval, grunts, and monosyllables. Very sparing of words, was Mr. Crowley. It was almost pitch black at this point, and I was getting hungry.

"'About seven o'clock the telephone rang and he asked me to answer it. It was my wife asking me to return at once to see an unexpected visitor. Finishing the conversation, I returned to my chair and, after I explained the call, Crowley nodded assent to my request to leave immediately.

"'On the way out, as the lights had not been turned on, I bumped my head, which explains this bruise. Just as I reached the door, he called after me— "See you tomorrow at ten." He was certainly all right when I left him shortly after seven.'

"Although Bronson's telephone alibi was later proved sound, he had hardly finished his story before I was convinced he was implicated," concluded Fordney.

◐ ◐ ◐

What directed suspicion to Bronson?

(solution on page 152)

The Poison Murder Case

"I'm going to the theater now," Bob Kewley told Professor Fordney at their club. "I wish you'd spend the evening with Uncle John. He's been worried lately."

Upon reaching the Kewley home an hour later, Fordney found the butler in an agitated state. "After ordering coffee, Mr. Kewley locked himself in his library an hour ago, sir. When I rapped on the door just now, he didn't answer."

The two men forced the lock and found John Kewley on the floor, an empty strychnine bottle at his side. The terrace door was open. After a careful examination, Fordney returned home. A few hours later, Bob Kewley entered his living room.

"Thought I'd stop in on my way home. Don't you think Uncle John looks worried?"

"Your uncle, Bob, is dead. Strychnine. Your butler and I found him lying on the floor, but were too late to save him."

"How horrible, Fordney! Why was the library door locked, do you suppose?"

"That puzzles me. Has your butler been with you long?"

"For years," replied Bob, his head buried in his hands.

"Well, you're a wealthy man now."

"What of it? Uncle John meant more to me than all the money in the world."

"I wish I could believe that," replied Fordney. "You'll need a better alibi than those," pointing to the ticket stubs Bob was nervously fingering.

❂ ❂ ❂

How had Kewley aroused the Professor's suspicions?

(solution on page 153)

A Strange "Kidnapping"

"I haven't the faintest idea why I was kidnapped," said Johnson to Professor Fordney, an hour after he returned home from his ordeal. "I never miss Sunday evening services, you know, so I'm afraid I haven't much time to discuss it now."

"Oh, just a brief account of your experience is all that is necessary," remarked the Professor.

So Johnson proceeded. "I was walking along Burnham Street about 2 a.m. Friday. I recall because I had just wound my watch. When two masked men, with drawn guns, ordered me into a blue sedan. I was blindfolded and gagged and my hands were tied. After they drove for about an hour, I was led into a house and down some stairs to a small room, where they removed my blindfold and gag. They took off my outer clothing and hung it on a chair. Then they questioned me at length about the Shirley case and refused to believe I knew nothing of it.

"Exasperated, they threatened to kill me, and when I protested, one of them hit me on the head with a heavy blackjack and I went down unconscious.

"The next thing I knew was when I came to this morning with a terrific headache. I lay still for a few minutes and, hearing nothing but the ticking of my watch, I cautiously got to my feet and groped for the door, as the room was in darkness. Before I could locate it, two men, still masked, entered, turned on the light, apologized profusely for the treatment I had received, and said they had mistaken me for someone else. Then they gave me something to eat, blindfolded me again, and drove me to within a block of my home, still apologizing for the mistake. Before I could remove my blindfold after getting out of the car, it had sped away.

"It's all very mysterious to me. I can't make anything of it."

"I won't give you away, Johnson," smiled the Professor. "Your wife undoubtedly believes your fable, but you'd better think up a better one the next time."

❍ ❍ ❍

What flaw did the Professor find in Johnson's story which proved the "kidnapping" was a fake?

(solution on page 153)

A Valuable Formula

"I had just stepped behind that screen near the door to wash my hands when a man, gun in hand, entered the room and stood motionless for a few seconds," said Hyde. "Apparently satisfied no one was here, he walked to the desk over there by the window. As he rummaged through the papers in the drawer, I hastily called Headquarters, leaving the receiver off the hook, trusting you would trace the call. I was afraid to speak when the operator answered because I was unarmed and he looked like a desperate fellow."

"You say he took nothing but a valuable formula from your desk?" inquired the Professor.

"That's all—he touched nothing else."

"Rather careless to leave such an important paper lying around like that, wasn't it?"

"Well, I suppose so, though it was only a copy. I sold the original to Schmitz yesterday for twenty thousand dollars and I intended to destroy the duplicate tonight."

"Would that formula be valuable to anyone else?"

"Yes, it would be worth twice as much to Schmitz's competitors."

"Why didn't you sell it to them in the first place, then?"

"Schmitz financed me while I was perfecting the formula, so I thought it only right to sell it to him, even though I could have gotten more for it from the other firm."

"As this is such a small, bright room and you observed so much through that crack in the screen," said Fordney sarcastically, "you should be able to give us a *very* good description of the intruder?

"Oh, I can do that," Hyde replied, with assurance. "He was a big fellow about six feet tall and weighed around two hundred pounds. He had jet-black hair and a scar on his face. As he left obviously unaware of my presence, I noticed he had a big rip in the back of his blue coat."

"Well, Hyde, as part of your story is incredible, you can't expect me to believe any of it."

○ ○ ○

Why does the Professor think Hyde's story is a lie?

(solution on page 154)

Strangled

66Twenty-two days of this awfully dry heat wave," groaned Professor Fordney. "I can't remember anything like it."

"Tell us about the Greer case, Professor," urged the rocking-chair brigade. "It'll take your mind off the heat."

"Well, you know the salient facts. The body of Irene Greer, lying beside the railroad crossing, was found half a mile from here by a fishing party at 6 a.m. the day before yesterday. It could be seen that she was a beautiful girl despite the tousled hair matted with mud and a nasty bruise on her cheek. Her sunny yellow dress was torn and dirty, but of the finest quality. She had on shoes, but the left heel was cracked.

"It looked as though she had been placed on the track with the expectation that she would be struck by a train and identification made impossible. No doubt she was unconscious when this was done, but she must have revived temporarily and crawled to the gravel before a train came along. There she died.

"Oddly, while her body was bruised and twisted, there were no marks on her throat to indicate strangulation, yet Dr. Bridewell says that was the cause of death.

"She was found in the middle of nowhere. Oh, yes, she was probably strangled with a scarf which, employed in a certain manner, would leave no outward trace.

"Now you folks should know how I learned Irene Greer was attacked elsewhere and then brought to the vicinity where she was found," smiled the Professor.

○ ○ ○

What does the Professor mean?

(solution on page 154)

Death in the Office

When Professor Fordney reached Gifford's office, he found a policeman already there.

"Gifford's dead," he was told. "What brings you here?"

"He telephoned me a few minutes ago. He said he had been shot, and then I had a hard time understanding him. This street is on your beat, isn't it?"

"Yes. I heard the shot when I was in Smith's cigar store. It took me a while to locate it. The door was locked and I had to break in."

As they walked into an inner office, they saw Gifford's body, a bullet through the heart, lying in a pool of blood.

Fordney stooped to pick up a revolver.

"It's an easy jump to the ground," observed the policeman, who was standing by an open window. "Did you know, sir," he added, "that Gifford has been troubled lately by blackmailers?"

"Yes. The last time I saw him, he told me he had been shot at a couple of weeks ago."

Fordney walked over to the door and found the lock was sprung, but the key still in it.

"I suppose," ventured the policeman, "that the blackmailers got him. They must have locked the door from the inside when they entered, shot him, and then jumped out the window."

"No," said Fordney, who was examining the key he had removed from the lock. "There weren't any murderers in here. Gifford committed suicide."

◍ ◍ ◍

Why was the Professor so sure it was suicide?

(solution on page 154)

They Usually Forget Something

"**H**ere is a good illustration of the old cliché that the smartest criminal leaves some clue in even the most carefully planned crime," mused Professor Fordney.

"While in Colshire, a beautiful little English village, I was asked by the local police to assist them in a rather puzzling affair.

"Suspicion of a particularly brutal murder had been directed toward an illiterate underworld character. He was accused of sending the following note found in the murdered man's pocket:

sir john

when i last seen you i sed i will kill you if the muney ain't here by mundy; all of it

yurs truly,
XX

"When Wellington, the Chief Constable, asked my opinion, I told him the writer of the note, and therefore probably the murderer, was obviously an educated man. After explaining why I was sure of that, he agreed with me.

"An odd sort of case. The murderer was found to be an extremely wealthy American whose sister had married the murdered man's brother."

"Well," laughed Bill Cargo, the man Fordney was speaking to. "It's a bit involved for me. I can't figure it out."

○ ○ ○

How did Forney know the American
suspect was educated?

(solution on page 155)

The Professor Gives a Lesson

Yesterday, Cardoni waltzed into into Inspector Kelley's office.

"I want to speak to you alone, Chief," Cardoni said, eyeing the Professor with frank suspicion.

"It's all right. Go ahead," said Kelley.

"I've got some information on the Curtis kidnappers. How much is it worth?"

"That all depends. Let's hear the story."

"They're in one of my old buildings, down on the East Side. Three men and a woman. All you've got to do, Chief, is to take this, walk in and surprise 'em," said our informer, tossing a Yale key on Kelley's desk. "They rented a room from me about a week ago."

"Sounds much too easy, Cardoni. I want something more definite than that. What makes you think they're the kidnappers?"

"I heard them having an argument as I was doing some repair work in the hall. One of the guys threatened to squeal if he didn't get a bigger cut. It sounded interestin', so I peeked through the keyhole. They were sittin' at a table in the middle of the room. It had a stack of money on it."

"Your story doesn't yet show they had any connection with the Curtis kidnapping," Kelley said.

"NO? Well, last night I heard them mention 'Curtis' several times. And that ain't all," continued Cardoni, with a triumphant air. "Here's a coded message one of them must have dropped. Well, Chief, how much do I get?"

"Get out!" hollered Kelley.

*   *   *

Why did Inspector Kelly treat the informer so rudely?

(solution on page 155)

Upstairs and Down

"Let's hear your story," said Inspector Kelley to Policeman Kirk, as Fordney dropped into a comfortable chair at Headquarters.

"The neighbors were worried because they hadn't seen old lady Brill about for a couple of days and asked me to investigate.

"Getting no answer to my phone call, I broke open the front door, ran upstairs, and I still didn't see her. So I ran down and through the hall, unlocked the kitchen door, and found her on the floor—with a bullet through her heart and a gun beside her. The windows and the doors to the porch and cellar were locked on the inside and nothing seemed to be disturbed.

"Looked like suicide to me. However, I learned her nephew was at the house yesterday about the time the doctor said she died, so I brought him in," concluded Kirk.

"Why did you run upstairs before examining the lower floor?" asked Kelley.

"Thought I heard a noise up there, sir," replied the policeman.

"Any fingerprints on the gun?" inquired Fordney.

"Just those of the old lady," answered Kelley.

"I have a key to the house," interrupted the nephew. "I went in yesterday, called to her, but she didn't answer, so I thought she'd gone out."

"Did you go upstairs?" asked the Professor.

"Yes, I ran up there, calling her name, but came right down again and left immediately."

"Well, Kelley, of course it's murder—as you probably know. I suppose you'll hold this fellow?"

"I certainly intend to," replied the Inspector.

◦ ◦ ◦

How did Fordney know the woman
had been murdered?

(solution on page 155)

Class Day

"**B**aklioff, in person, combined with the film *Grand Hotel*, had packed the Paramount," said the Professor. "Every seat was occupied and standing-room was at a premium. What an opening it was!" he continued.

"As the film neared its end and the orchestra reached the climax of Mascagni's 'Cavalleria Rusticana' (under the magnificent leadership of Baklioff), a shot rang out.

"Inspector Kelley, who accompanied me, was immediately on his feet bellowing, 'Lights!' They were quickly turned on and the film stopped. Warning everyone to keep his seat, we started for the back of the theater, when a man's body slumped out of a seat and fell almost at our feet. A hurried examination disclosed he had been shot in the back of the head and that he was an extremely tall man.

"Leaving Kelley to look after things, I hurried to the operator's booth. When almost there, I heard another shot and knew I was too late. Entering the small compartment, hung under the balcony, I found the operator with a bullet through his temple and a smoking revolver by his side.

"'Not much to this,' I remarked, as Kelley joined me.

"'I wonder if he got the right man,' commented the Inspector. 'I don't understand how he could have made such a splendid shot under the circumstances. Amazing!'"

"Was the dead man sitting in an aisle seat?" interrupted one of the class.

"Yes," replied Fordney.

"Gee, that's a good one, Professor, but I know now the one thing wrong with your story," said the student.

⊙ ⊙ ⊙

Do you?

(solution on page 156)

A Hot Pursuit

"**H**ello, Smith," said Professor Fordney as he opened the door. "What's up?"

"Uncle Fred's house has been robbed. He had some negotiable bonds in the library safe and told me to stick close to home until he returned from New York."

"Were they stolen?" interrogated Fordney.

"I'm afraid so. I was up in my bedroom about twenty minutes ago when I heard a noise. I rushed downstairs just in time to see a man dash out of the library. I ran after him and, as I passed the door, I noticed the safe was open, so I suppose he got the bonds. He jumped into a waiting automobile and I trailed him in my car which, fortunately, was standing in front of the house. But he got away from me."

"Did you get his license plate?"

"No. Couldn't see it. When I lost him in the traffic, I drove right over here."

"Didn't you keep the house locked while you were upstairs?"

"Yes, but the burglar chiseled open a cellar window."

"Well, let's go over and have a look," suggested Fordney.

When they reached the Smith home, they found the bonds gone.

"Did you lock the front door when you ran out of the house?"

"Why—er," replied Smith nervously, "the door locks automatically. I don't know what Uncle Fred will say when he gets back."

"He'll say plenty if you tell him the story you told me," interrupted the Professor. "I suggest you put the bonds back."

❂ ❂ ❂

Where did Smith make his incriminating slip?

(solution on page 156)

A Question of Identity

Professor Fordney and three of his friends were enjoying their weekly get-together at the University Club.

"Professor," said Patrie, "tell us something about that Yelpir murder case you were working on."

"Well, gentlemen," he replied, in his retiring manner, "as you know, Yelpir's affairs were common knowledge, and the fact that several women had reasons to wish him dead complicated matters a bit.

"His body was found in his study, which opened onto a corridor. At the opposite end of the corridor was a staircase that led to the servants' quarters above.

"Diana Lane, a houseguest of Mrs. Yelpir at the time of the murder, was questioned, and she appeared nervous. She insisted, however, that she had been in her room at the time Yelpir was slain.

"Nora, a servant, testified that as she was descending the stairs leading from the servants' quarters at midnight, she saw Diana Lane nearing the other end of the hallway toward Yelpir's room. She identified Miss Lane by her famous emerald pendant and noted that she was dressed in an enticing black negligée. She followed a minute later and heard Diana and Yelpir violently quarreling. Upon returning to the servants' quarters, Nora heard a shot as she opened the door of her room.

"In the face of such evidence, Miss Lane admitted having gone to the study at the time, but protested her innocence, declaring she had remained only a minute.

"While Miss Lane was acquitted, you know, her reputation was not above reproach. Even so, I knew without further investigation that Nora's testimony was maliciously false."

❂ ❂ ❂

How did the Professor know?

(solution on page 156)

A Yachtsman's Alibi

"I've often remarked," said Professor Fordney, "how very difficult it is to fake an alibi without someone's assistance. A case in point is a messy affair we cleared up recently.

"I didn't definitely suspect Picus when I happened to bump into him at the Fourth-of-July parade, the morning after an acquaintance of his had been found dead under suspicious circumstances. I rather casually asked him where he had been and what he had been doing the previous afternoon about four o'clock, the apparent time of the man's death. He related the following story:

"'I took my sailboat out about noon yesterday. It was great on the water. Around three o'clock, however, when I was perhaps ten miles out, the wind died down completely. There wasn't a breath of air, and I knew that, unless I could attract some boat, I was in for an uncomfortable time. Remembering that the international distress signal is a flag flown upside down, I ran mine up to the top of the mast in that manner. Thank God it was a clear day.

"'In about an hour, the steamer *Leone* hove to, and I went aboard her after securing my boat with a towline. The captain said he had seen my distress signal about four miles away and would put me ashore at Gladsome Landing. He did so, and, as there was no one about, I hailed a passing motorist who gave me a lift back to town. Imagine my surprise when I read in the paper this morning that the *Leone* had been sunk in a storm after putting me ashore, and all hands had been lost!'

"While I knew," remarked the Professor, "that the *Leone* had been sunk with all on board, after hearing Picus's story I immediately arrested him on suspicion of murder."

◦ ◦ ◦

What's wrong with Picus's alibi?

(solution on page 157)

Murder at Coney Island

Inspector Kelley and Professor Fordney were seated in Kelley's office when Policeman Fanning and his charge entered. After Fanning's hurried explanation, Jasper told his story:

"I'm the ticket taker on a merry-go-round at Coney Island. This bein' Saturday, we had a big crowd. The trip was almost over when I reached out, saying, 'Ticket, please,' and I see this woman sittin' up in the middle of the chariot with that terrible look on her face. She didn't answer, and when I shook her, she slumped over in the corner. I screamed, jumped off, and ran for the manager. I got blood on my hand when I shook her.

"Yes, sir, she'd ridden a couple of times and I seen the man she was with on the two rides before," continued Jasper, giving a detailed description of him. "I happened to see him jump off just before I got to her."

"The doctor said she had been stabbed through the heart and had died instantly?" queried Professor Fordney.

"That's right, sir," replied the policeman.

"It seems strange, Jasper," remarked the Professor, "that you can give such a good description of this woman's companion on two previous rides when you just 'happened' to notice him jump off. Does the merry-go-round ever make you dizzy?"

"No, sir; I'm used to it."

"Well, Inspector," said Fordney, turning to his friend, "I suppose you are going to hold this man?"

"Certainly," replied Kelley. "That's just about the dizziest story I've heard in a long time."

○ ○ ○

What justified the police in holding Jasper?

(solution on page 157)

Too Clever

"**R**eceiving no reply to my ring and finding the door unlocked, I went in," said Albert Lynch.

"Dawson was seated at his desk shot through the head. Seeing he was dead, I called the police and remained here."

"Touch anything, Lynch?" asked Professor Fordney.

"No, sir, nothing."

"Positive of that, are you?"

"Absolutely, sir."

The Professor made a careful examination of the desk and found Dawson had been writing a letter. At the bottom of the letter, and covered by the dead man's hand, was a penned message: "A. L. did thi——" and weakly trailed off.

Further examination disclosed several kinds of writing paper, a pen tray holding the recently used pen, inkwell, eraser, stamps, letters, and bills. The gun used to fire the shot was on the floor by the side of the chair, and the bullet was found embedded in the chaise longue.

After a few questions, Fordney was quickly convinced of Lynch's innocence.

"What do you make of it, Professor?" inquired Inspector Kelley.

"Though the scrawled note certainly looks like Dawson's writing, I am sure an expert will find it isn't. I'm not surprised to find the gun free of prints. Pretty thorough job, this. Good thing for you, Lynch, and for us too, that the murderer was careless about something."

"Right," said Kelley. "But you aren't such a wise old owl, Fordney. This is like the Morrow case we handled. Remember?"

"Good for you, Inspector," laughed the Professor.

○ ○ ○

How did both men so quickly determine that the incriminating note had not been left by Dawson?

(solution on page 158)

Bloody Murder

"**A** bad mess, this," said Professor Fordney to Sergeant Reynolds, as they viewed the bloody scene.

"Yeah, I wish these guys wouldn't be quite so thorough when they bump themselves off," replied Reynolds as he set grimly to work.

A man with his throat cut, the head almost severed, sat slumped over a blood-spattered desk. What a horrible sight! His bloodstained coat flung across the room, the razor! the shirt! the tie! his hands! covered with blood, made a ghastly picture framed by the flickering light of a dying candle.

After turning on the lights, Fordney bent down to take a closer look at the man.

"His face seems vaguely familiar, Sergeant, but I can't recall at the moment where I've seen him. How long has he been dead, Doctor?"

"About two hours," replied the coroner.

At this moment the telephone rang. The caller, upon hearing Fordney's voice, immediately disconnected.

"Odd," murmured the Professor as he hung up the receiver. "I remember now where I saw this man. His name is Thompson."

As he glanced around, he observed that the alarm clock on the dresser had stopped just two hours and fifteen minutes before.

The telephone rang again and Fordney motioned Reynolds to answer.

"Hello!" he said. "Mr. Thompson stepped out for a few minutes. Leave your number. I'll have him call you." The man at the other end inquired who was speaking and, when Reynolds replied, "A friend," he hung up.

"Better trace that call, Sergeant; this is murder," said Fordney.

"What!" exclaimed Reynolds. "Still looks like suicide to me!"

❂ ❂ ❂

Do you agree with Reynolds or the Professor? Why?

(solution on page 158)

Death, Backstage

Claudia Mason, the beautiful and popular young actress, was found lying across the chaise longue in her elaborately furnished dressing room, dead from a bullet wound in the temple.

She had sold her jewels and, with a heroic gesture, partially paid her many debts. Sergeant Reynolds picked up the discharged revolver lying next to Claudia's right hand, and after careful examination said:

"No fingerprints, of course. Gosh, Fordney, look at the two rocks she didn't sell," he exclaimed, pointing to a large emerald on her left hand and a diamond on her right.

"Call Maria, her maid. I want to find out who this fellow is," said the Professor, nodding toward a man's photograph signed, Juan. "This was evidently addressed to him," he said, passing over a note that read:

Dear Juan,

I am so despondent. The money from my jewels was not nearly enough.

Claudia

"Not many of these dames kill themselves over their debts," muttered Reynolds as he went to call Maria.

The maid entered the room, sobbing and hysterical.

"Who is Juan?" asked Professor Fordney.

"He's the leading man in the show."

"Why wasn't this note delivered to him?"

"I forgot it."

"You found her?"

"Yes. When I came to help her dress she—was—like that!"

"Is Juan in his dressing room now?"

"I believe so."

When Reynolds brought him into Claudia's room, he dropped to his knees beside the dead girl.

"My God! She's killed herself!"

"No, she hasn't, young man. She was murdered," said the Professor.

○ ○ ○

Why was he sure it was not suicide?

(solution on page 158)

An Easy Combination

"**I** was working late, preparing an advertising campaign," continued Fellows, the man Professor Fordney had been questioning. "About ten-fifteen, I heard the outer office door click. Being unarmed, I hurriedly turned out the lights in my office and waited breathlessly, as there was a large sum of money in the safe. I knew my chances of attracting attention from the tenth floor were small. I grabbed the telephone and I hastily dialed Headquarters and told them in a low voice to send help immediately. Then, creeping noiselessly to the open safe, I gently shut the door, twirled the combination, and crawled behind that big old-fashioned desk.

"Shortly afterward the robber entered my office, flashed his light over the place, and went to the safe. He had it open in a few minutes, took the money, and left. That's all I know about it."

"What time is it now, Mr. Fellows?" inquired Fordney.

"Why, I haven't a watch."

"How, then, did you know it was about ten-fifteen when you heard the door click?"

"I had gone next door for a sandwich. As I left, I glanced at the restaurant clock and noticed it was five past ten. I had been back about five minutes," replied Fellows.

"You say the burglar was masked," continued the Professor. "How did you know it?"

"As he focused his flashlight on the combination and bent over, I saw the mask," returned Fellows belligerently.

"Very interesting," smiled Fordney, "but you'll have to be a better liar than that, Fellows, to fool me."

○ ○ ○

Where did the Professor detect the lie?

(*solution on page 159*)

A Modern Knight

66 "There was hardly a breath of air as we sat on the terrace enjoying tea," reminisced Professor Fordney. "Rocca excused himself, saying he wished to telephone. Shortly after he entered the house, we heard a shot. I rushed into the drawing room and found Rocca, smoking gun in hand, staring dumbly at the chair in front of the open window that held the huddled body of Chase.

"A quick examination disclosed the telephone receiver off the hook, a single cigarette stub of Rocca's brand in the ashtray, a bullet hole in the gauze curtain six inches below the windowsill, and Rocca's open cigarette case in Chase's lap. His replies to my hastily put questions were evasive. Inspector Kelley arrived while I was talking and took up the questioning.

"'Did you use the telephone?'

"'Yes.'

"'You came directly to this room and did not leave it?'

"'Yes.'

"'Chase was engaged to your sister?'

"'Yes, he was.'

"'Did you offer Chase a cigarette?'

"'I did.'

"'How did that dent get in your cigarette case?'

"'I dropped it about a week ago.'

"'Did you shoot Chase?'

"'I refuse to answer that question.'

"At this point the doctor arrived and located the bullet in Chase's body. Rocca then admitted Chase had been shot with the gun found in his own hand, but stubbornly refused to say anything more.

"'What's your opinion, Professor?' Kelley asked.

"'Well,' I replied, 'Rocca is obviously shielding someone. We have positive proof he came directly here and has not left this room. That, combined with the other evidence discovered, absolutely exonerates Rocca.'"

◉ ◉ ◉

How did the Professor know Rocca
had not shot Chase?

(solution on page 159)

The Jewel Robbery

"**Y**ou say that as your butler called for help after you left, a stranger, by the name of Dudley, was passing the house and rushed in?"

"That's right," Owings corroborated, as the two men sat in Fordney's study. "It was rather late last Friday evening before I was ready to leave town for the weekend, and as Stuben, the butler, wasn't feeling well, I told him to stay upstairs and that I would lock up when I left.

"I had some diamonds in the safe, so he said he wouldn't leave the house until I returned later in the weekend," continued Owings.

"About eleven that night, he heard a humming noise and, having the diamonds in mind, ran downstairs to investigate. Finding the wall safe open and the jewels gone, he let out a scream for help.

"Stuben has been with me for years, Professor, and I have implicit faith in him."

"Did Dudley see anyone leave?" asked Fordney.

"No; the robber or robbers must have left by the back door,

as Dudley was right in front of the house when he heard Stuben's call for help," replied Owings. "Both men say the room smelled of cigarette smoke, so the burglars must have just left."

"Was the back door unlocked?" inquired the Professor.

"No, it was closed. It has a device which locks it automatically from the outside when it's pulled to."

"Well, you'd better swear out a warrant for your butler and Dudley," said Fordney. "I'm sure they know where your diamonds are. Long service, you know, isn't necessarily a pledge of loyalty."

○ ○ ○

Why did Fordney so advise Owings?

(solution on page 159)

Before the Coroner's Inquest

"**L**et's run over your testimony before the inquest opens," said Fordney.

"All right," replied Curry.

"About three-thirty on Thursday, I got into the boat in front of my cottage and rowed upstream. About fifty yards below the bridge, I looked up and saw Scott and Dawson going across it in opposite directions. As the two men passed, Scott reached out, grabbed Dawson, and hit him in the jaw. Then he pulled a gun. In the scuffle that followed, Scott fell off the bridge and dropped into the water. The current was strong, so by the time I reached the spot, he had sunk. When I finally pulled him into the boat, he was dead."

"Was it a clear day?" asked Fordney.

"Well, it had been showering early in the afternoon, but the sun was shining then."

"Are you positive Scott got that bruise by hitting his head on the rocks when he fell? The prosecution, you know, is going to claim that Dawson hit him on the head with something, then deliberately pushed him off the bridge," commented Fordney.

"I *know* he got that bruise on the rocks," stated Curry emphatically.

"All right," said the Professor, "but I don't think the jury will believe you. Personally, I'm sure Dawson didn't intentionally kill Scott, but we'll have to have better proof than that if we hope to acquit him.

"By the way," he continued, "be sure to state you knew of the grudge Scott bore Dawson."

❁ ❁ ❁

Why was the Professor doubtful the coroner's jury would believe Curry's testimony?

(solution on page 160)

The Fifth Avenue Holdup

"What's the hurry?" asked Professor Fordney, as Baldwin collided with him in the doorway of the office at the back of the exclusive Cross Jewelry Store.

"I—I—was going to help search for the robbers," stammered Baldwin as he backed into the office.

"Well, tell me what happened first," said Fordney, as Dr. Lyman, coroner, knelt beside Mr. Cross.

"There's the special safe for the emerald behind that miniature portrait. I was in here when Mr. Cross entered with two gentlemen," exclaimed Baldwin nervously.

"He asked me to bring in a tray of diamonds. I set it on the table—both men pulled guns and as Cross protested, one of them knocked him unconscious with a blow on the head. The other forced me into that chair saying, 'All right, buddy. We'll wait on ourselves.' Then he put the diamonds in his pocket. I'm thankful I'm alive. I telephoned Headquarters, then rushed out into the store, but they had escaped," concluded Baldwin.

"So they got away with the famous Cross emerald, eh?"

"Yes. The safe door was slightly open. Mr. Cross tried to call my attention to it with a jerk of his thumb as the robber pocketed the diamonds. Otherwise they wouldn't have discovered it."

"How is he, Doctor?" asked Fordney.

"He'll never come to, I'm afraid. Those two blows on the head were a bit too much for him."

"Two blows!" burst Fordney. "Are you sure, Baldwin, you weren't hurrying away with the emerald? I'm not!"

○ ○ ○

Why did Fordney think Baldwin had stolen the emerald?

(solution on page 160)

Behind Locked Doors

At the spotless Collingham home, Professor Fordney found Clive Kingston, the Judge's nephew, and Watkins, the butler, greatly alarmed. Forcing open the library door that had been locked for three months, they saw the Judge seated in front of the fireplace opposite the door, quite dead.

"Wait!" called Professor Fordney to Watkins, who had rushed into the room.

"He's all right," said Kingston, as he and Fordney halted over the threshold.

"Perhaps, but I don't want any clues obliterated. Come back carefully and get us a couple of small rugs, Watkins," commanded Fordney.

Walking only on the rugs placed over the thick, plain carpet, Fordney and Kingston reached the Judge's side and found him dead—shot through the heart.

Kingston called the Professor's attention to footprints in the carpet near the fireplace. As he fitted his shoe to an impression, he said, "These are mine, and those, of course, must be Watkins's."

"Throw me your shoe," called Fordney to the butler, standing in the doorway. "Yes, these are yours all right, and I can see the third set was made by the Judge—notice the impression left by his peculiarly constructed right shoe."

"There's the gun under the table," called the butler.

"Pretty sharp eyes, Watkins," said the Professor, picking up and critically examining the gun. "No fingerprints, of course," he mused.

"Look!" exclaimed Kingston. "The glass in that picture is broken. Were two shots fired?"

"Only one," said Fordney, as with great care he picked the Judge's nose glasses from his lap where they had fallen, unbroken. "I think I know now who murdered your uncle."

○ ○ ○

Whom did Fordney suspect, and why?

(solution on page 160)

Lost at Sea

"Tell us exactly what happened," said Professor Fordney as he sat in his study with Mrs. Rollins.

"It was a dark, moonless night. I couldn't see a thing. At twelve o'clock, when we were about ten miles off Point Breeze, I retired to my cabin, leaving my husband on deck. We were alone on the boat.

"In a few minutes, hearing loud shouts, I joined him again. We could hear a boat approaching, running without lights, as were we. My husband told me to return to the cabin, which I did.

"Soon after doing so, a bump, trampling feet, and loud swearing told me our visitors had come aboard. I went up and, just as I stepped on deck, a man put a gun against my ribs and told me to keep quiet. I heard my husband engaged in a terrific fight with two others in front of me.

"They must have known he always carried that leather bag of loose diamonds. When he dropped it in the fight, I saw one of them picked it up from the deck.

"They finally knocked him unconscious and took him to their

boat after binding and gagging me. As you know, I was found drifting next morning by that fisherman."

"How was your husband dressed?" inquired Fordney.

"It was very hot—he had no shirt on, but wore dark trousers."

"Shoes or tennis slippers?"

"Why—shoes, of course," replied Mrs. Rollins with noticeable hesitation.

"Well," said Fordney tersely, "it's amazing to me that you expect to collect insurance on your diamonds on such a flimsy story. You and your husband will be lucky if you aren't prosecuted."

◦ ◦ ◦

Where did the elaborate story fall down?

(solution on page 161)

A Suave Gunman

"Can you describe this fellow?" asked Professor Fordney of Henry Taylor, manager of the National Theater.

"Yes. He was a tall, well-dressed, good-looking chap. Wore a panama hat, turned-down brim, blue coat, smart blue tie, white flannels with a silver belt-buckle, black-and-white sport shoes, and had a general air of culture and refinement."

"Just what did he do?"

"As I was counting the receipts, he came into the office, gun in hand, and commanded me to get up from the desk and move over by that table.

"After putting the money in a briefcase he carried, he took out a cigarette and asked me to light it for him, still covering me, of course.

"Then he gagged me and tied me to the chair. He then opened the door, looked cautiously around, came back and, with a quiet 'sorry' and a warning, turned and left. As he passed through the door, he unbuttoned his coat and slipped the revolver into his back pocket. The show was just letting out, so I suppose he mingled with the crowd and escaped," Taylor concluded.

"Are you insured against this loss of eight thousand dollars?" inquired Fordney.

"Yes."

"Could you see the color of the bandit's hair?"

"It was blond."

"Anything unusual about him?"

"No. Except that he was constantly clearing his throat in a peculiar manner," replied Taylor.

"Left- or right-handed?"

"Why—I'm not sure. Right-handed, though, I think."

"This has gone far enough, Taylor," said Fordney sharply. "The robbery was obviously faked by you."

○ ○ ○

How did Fordney know Taylor had faked the holdup?

(solution on page 161)

Accidental Death.

Returning to town late one night, Professor Fordney was driving along an unfrequented road when the sight of a motorcycle policeman examining a car in a ditch caused him to stop and offer his services. Joining the policeman, he found that a man, obviously the driver, had been thrown through the windshield and was lying about six feet from the car.

His examination disclosed that the man had been terribly cut about the head. The jugular vein was completely severed. The bent steering wheel, shattered glass, and the blood on the front seat and floor of the car were unspoken evidence of the tragedy.

Fordney also noted the speedometer had stopped at 62.

A search of the body revealed nothing unusual except that the man wore only one glove. The other could not be found. The Professor was pondering this when the policeman handed him his report of accidental death, saying, "Is that how you see it, sir?"

"I think," replied Fordney slowly, "you'd better change that to murder. In the absence of any further evidence, it seems to be pretty clearly indicated."

"Murder!" exclaimed the bewildered policeman. "I don't understand how you make that out."

After explaining his reason and with a final admonition to continue a careful search for the missing glove, the Professor returned to his car and drove down the wide, smooth highway toward home and a good night's rest.

Fordney's deduction was confirmed when the missing glove and the murderer were found.

○ ○ ○

How had he arrived at his startling conclusion?

(solution on page 161)

Easy Money

"**M**r. Walker hurried into the kitchen," said the valet to Professor Fordney, "and told me he was called away unexpectedly and that I was to go to his library and take the money he had won last night to the bank.

"I was busy," he continued, "but in about five minutes I went through the hall, and, thinking I heard a noise, I stopped and listened at the study door. There was someone moving about. The door was open. As I peered around it, I saw a masked man, gun in hand, hesitating near the fireplace.

"Then he went over to the table in the center of the room, picked up the stacks of ten- and twenty-dollar bills, and left by the window. I called the police immediately and gave them a description."

"Exactly what time was that?" asked Fordney.

"Just about ten o'clock, sir."

"Had you been in the library before that, this morning?"

"No, I hadn't."

"Were you in your Mr. Walker's room today?"

"No. What's that got to do with it?"

"Nothing," murmured Fordney, "nothing at all! Does your employer gamble often?"

"I don't think so."

"How much did he win last night?"

"He didn't say."

"Humph," said Fordney, as he pointed to a bill on the floor, "the thief dropped one. I see this is quite a library," he continued, glancing around the large, beautifully furnished room. "Do you read much, Wilkins?"

"A bit, sir."

"Did you ever read, 'Honesty is the best policy'?"

❂ ❂ ❂

Why did the Professor think Wilkins had robbed his employer, Mr. Walker?

(solution on page 162)

Robbery at High Noon

"I wonder who had the nerve to commit such a robbery at high noon," mused Professor Fordney as he examined the safe, seventeen minutes after it had been rifled. "Same old story: no fingerprints, no evidence."

"Found anything?" asked Lawson nervously as he entered his drawing room.

"Not yet. Are you here alone, Lawson?"

"No. John, my nephew, is staying with me. Everyone else is in town."

"Where is he now?"

"Oh, he left about an hour ago."

At 3:20 p.m. Fordney noticed Jones, the gardener, working at the edge of a flower bed. He kept looking furtively at the house while he frantically covered over the hole he had dug. Finishing, he hurriedly walked toward the boat landing.

Fordney, following, reached the dock just as John guided his motorboat in.

"Have a nice day?" asked Fordney.

"Yep. Had a grand run up the lakes."

"Where were you when your uncle's safe was robbed?"

"I was hauling in a big muskie! What a battle he gave me! See him at the end of the boat? Isn't he a beauty?"

"When did you return?" demanded Fordney of the gardener.

"I don't know what time it was," he replied nervously, glancing at John.

"You must have some idea."

"Well, it was about noon," he reluctantly answered.

"By the way, John, do you know the combination of your uncle's safe?" inquired Fordney.

"Is that old weasel accusing me?"

"No, he isn't. But I've got my suspicions!"

Ø Ø Ø

Whom did Fordney suspect and why?

(solution on page 162)

The Wrong Foot Forward

"The witness says," explained the interpreter, "that as the trolley came to a sudden stop, the conductor ran to the front and yelled to the motorman, 'You've done it again.'"

The man on the witness stand looked bewildered and frightened.

"He further says that there were two sailors in the trolley and that they jumped off and ran."

"Have they been located yet?" inquired the Judge.

"No, Your Honor; we've been unable to trace them, although the conductor gave a good description," replied counsel.

"Proceed."

The interpreter continued.

"Paslovsky, the witness, declares he had a clear view of the plaintiff when he got off. He states that just as the plaintiff put his foot on the ground, with his back to the front of the car, it gave a sudden start and he was thrown to the road."

"Could the witness tell the court about that in his own words?" asked the Judge.

"No, Your Honor; his English is limited."

"Continue."

"Paslovsky," declared the interpreter, "says he picked up this picture from the floor of the trolley—a snapshot of a sailor and a girl."

"Case dismissed," thundered the Judge, "and don't ever bring another like that into this court."

◦ ◦ ◦

Why was His Honor justified in so abruptly dismissing the suit for damages? asked Professor Fordney of his class in criminology.

(solution on page 163)

Death Attends the Party

"He had a big party last night," said Graves, the valet. "Certainly looks like it," retorted Professor Fordney. He surveyed the crazily balanced glasses, overflowing ashtrays, and liquor rings on the small, fragile antique table at which Carlton Dawes sat.

"It was awful, sir. Just as I turned to say 'good night' to him, he lifted his revolver, fired, and toppled over."

"Funny," mused Fordney. "He had everything to live for."

"Everything but the thing he wanted," replied the valet. "Madeline, his former wife, was here last night. He is always despondent after seeing her."

"Well, Graves, pretty nice for you, eh? How much did he leave you?"

"Ten thousand dollars, sir."

Fordney leaned over to examine the wound in Dawes's left temple. His head rested on the edge of the table, his right hand on his knee and his left hung lifelessly at his side.

"Anything been touched since the tragedy?"

"No, sir."

Fordney picked up Dawes's revolver where it had apparently fallen from his hand. After examining it and finding only the dead man's fingerprints, he laid it on the table. As he did so, Madeline entered the room. She stopped, horrified.

"What—what—has happened?"

"Where did you come from?" demanded Fordney.

"I've been upstairs. I didn't leave with the guests."

"Humph—you should have," as he shot her a quizzical look. "Your ex-husband was murdered."

Madeline slipped to the floor in a dead faint.

○ ○ ○

What convinced Fordney it was murder?

(solution on page 163)

No Way Out

On a battered desk in the small, dark room lay a penciled note in handwriting resembling that of the dead man:

Dear John,

You know the trouble I'm in. There's only one way out and I'm taking it. You're my pal and will understand. Good luck.

Paul

The only other furniture consisted of the chair in which Paul Morrow had been found with his throat cut, a bed, and a highly ornate and apparently brand-new wastebasket. It had been definitely established that the dead man had not left the room during the twenty-four hours before he was discovered.

Finishing his examination of the contents of the man's pockets—two twenty-dollar bills, a cheap watch, and an expensive wallet in which there was a picture of a beautiful woman—Fordney turned his attention to the meager inventory of the room.

"That's all we can find," said Inspector Kelley, indicating a dictionary, scraps of a letter in feminine handwriting found in the ornate wastebasket, a pen, some cheap stationery, a few clothes, pipe and tobacco, and a bloody, razor-sharp knife. "Certainly has all the appearances of suicide," he continued. "This door was locked and no one could have left by that window. What do you make of it, Fordney?"

The Professor didn't reply at once. He picked up the photograph, studied it a moment, and then, with a slow, searching look around the small room, said:

"Better try to piece those bits of letter together. This isn't suicide; it's murder."

"I believe you're right," exclaimed Kelley, with dawning comprehension.

ø ø ø

What brought Fordney to this conclusion?

(solution on page 163)

Midnight Murder

"**W**ho are you, and what's this all about?" demanded Inspector Kelley, as he and Professor Fordney arrived at the apartment in answer to a call.

"I'm Jack Day. I share this apartment with Al Quale. I returned from the theater, shortly after midnight, went into his room, and found him lying there on the bed. When I saw he was dead, I called Headquarters at once. God, this is terrible!"

"Those your things on the bed?" asked Kelley, indicating a bloodstained scarf, a hat, gloves, and cane.

"Yes, I tossed them there before I rushed to the telephone. Got that blood on the scarf when I bent over him."

"What time did you leave here this evening?"

"Shortly before seven," replied Day.

"Can you prove you were at the theater all evening?" demanded Kelley.

"Why, yes, I went with a friend."

"He's been dead about six hours, Inspector," said the coroner, finishing his examination at this point. "A deep knife wound, below the heart."

As Fordney picked up an earring from the floor, Day exclaimed: "Why, that belongs to his fiancée."

"Well, there'll be no wedding bells for him," remarked Kelley, with a start as he discovered that Day's cane was a sword with a long, thin, shining blade.

"Any blood, Inspector?" asked Fordney.

"None. Clean as a whistle."

"Well, Day, looks mighty bad for you," stated the Professor. "I don't know yet whether you killed him with that cane, or whether you killed him at all, but I do know you were here a few minutes after he was stabbed."

❂ ❂ ❂

How did the Professor know?

(solution on page 164)

Speakeasy Stickup

"I had counted the cash, and as I was working the combination to open the wall safe I heard this guy in back of me say, 'Get 'em up. This is a stickup.' I reached for the ceiling as he says, 'Make a move and I'll drill you!' He didn't sound like he was foolin', so I kept quiet.

"Well, he comes over, gives me a prod with his gun, pockets the dough, and asks me where the best liquor is, saying he don't want no bar whiskey either. I told him and I hear him pour himself a drink.

"Then he got real sociable-like, but wouldn't let me take my hands down. He kept on talkin' and makin' wisecracks, but finally got tired, I guess.

"With a warnin' that, if I moved before I could count twenty, my wife would be a widow, he beat it," concluded Sullivan.

"How much did he take?" inquired Professor Fordney, who had entered the speakeasy after hearing the bartender's call for help.

"About five hundred dollars," Sullivan replied. "We had a good day."

"Haven't you a gun here?"

"Sure, but I didn't have a chance. I ain't exactly no boy scout, but this guy was too big and tough-lookin' for me to tackle."

"How did you get that cut on your hand?" inquired the Professor. "And that bruise on your finger?"

"Opening a case of lemons," answered Sullivan.

"Well," said Fordney, "if your whiskey isn't any better than your attempt at a fake holdup, I'll have ginger ale."

○ ○ ○

How did Fordney know the stickup was a fake?

(solution on page 164)

Behind Time

Professor Fordney, on his way to investigate a case of blackmail, was musing on the perversity of human nature when a jolt threw him into the aisle as the train came to a sudden stop. Jumping off, he rushed ahead of the engine, where he found a small crowd gathered about the mutilated body of a man hit by the train. He was identified by a card in his pocket as John Nelson, an important figure in railroad labor circles.

"How did it happen?" inquired Fordney.

"Well," replied Morton, the engineer, "I was running twelve minutes late when I hit him. There are several miles of straight-away along here and I was beating it along at sixty miles trying to make up time. Didn't see him until we were about ten yards away, right on top of him. I jammed on the brakes, of course, but it was too late."

"Did you leave New York on time?"

"Yes, sir. One-thirty exactly."

"Why were you running late?"

"We were held up for about fifteen minutes outside of New Haven."

"What was your fireman doing when you hit this man?"

"Stoking the boiler."

"You say it was just a few seconds after four-thirty when you hit him?" demanded the Professor.

"That's right," agreed Morton.

"Did you know this man by any chance?"

"Yes, slightly—he was an officer in my union," replied the engineer, with a worried look.

"Well," said Fordney, "I don't know your object in telling such a story, or how you hoped to get away with it—you won't."

○ ○ ○

What justified Fordney in recommending Morton's arrest?

(solution on page 164)

A Broken Engagement

"**P**eculiar," murmured Fordney, as he examined the desk on which lay seven letters ready for mailing, three gray, one lavender, two pink, and one lemon-colored.

As he idly shaped the wax of the candle standing on the desk, he continued to ponder this unusual choice of color in stationery.

One of the letters was addressed to Dot Dalton, who had been murdered between eleven-forty and eleven-fifty. She was one of the guests at this house party in the Adirondacks.

All the letters were closed with black sealing wax stamped with the letter "F."

At midnight, Fordney began his questioning.

"What time did you retire?" he asked Molly Fleming, in whose bedroom he was seated.

"About ten," she replied.

"Was your door locked?"

"Yes."

"Hear any disturbance?"

"No; I was tired, fell asleep almost immediately, and didn't awaken until you knocked on my door a few minutes ago and told me of the tragedy."

"Why did you write to Dot?"

"I didn't see her last night and knew she intended leaving early this morning. Jack Fahey broke our engagement yesterday and told me he was going to marry Dot. My letter was to tell her just how despicable I thought she was in luring him away from me. He didn't love her. Of course, I'm sorry she's dead, but a lot of wives will feel safer."

"Why the various colors of stationery?" inquired the Professor.

"Oh, I always write in a color that seems to reflect the personality of my correspondent."

"I see,' said Fordney; "but unless you have a better alibi you'll be held under serious suspicion."

○ ○ ○

Why was the Professor practically certain Molly was involved in this horrible murder?

(solution on page 165)

The Holden Road Murder

"**W**hat a night!" sighed Professor Fordney as he hung up the telephone receiver. Half an hour later, still grumbling, he splashed his way through the mud and rain to the door of 27 Holden Road. Removing his boots in the spotless vestibule, he stepped into a large, well-furnished living room running the entire width of the house. Introducing himself and explaining he would question everyone later, he asked to be left alone.

In the far corner of the room, he found a man lying on the floor with his throat cut. As he bent over, his attention was attracted to a dime lying about five feet from the head of the dead man. He picked it up, regarded it curiously, and, with a thoughtful look, put it in his pocket. The Professor began his questioning with the butler.

"You found the dead man?"

"Yes, sir, I was returning from posting a letter about thirty minutes ago. Just as I was coming up the path of the front door,

I heard a scream, dashed in, and found Mr. White here gasping his last breath."

"Lose a dime?" inquired Fordney mildly.

"Why, I don't think so, sir," replied the butler nervously.

"I heard the scream from upstairs," volunteered Cannon, owner of the house, "and ran in here right behind Wilkins."

"Did either of you leave this room before I arrived?"

"No," replied Cannon; "we stayed here until you came."

"Did you, Mr. Cannon, lose a dime? No? Well," remarked Fordney, "it looks like collusion to me and I can tell you Inspector Kelley won't swallow this story."

○ ○ ○

What was wrong with the story?

(solution on page 165)

Fisherman's Luck

"**H**aving these stones in my possession, Professor Fordney, isn't proof that I had any part in the Morris robbery."

"I know all about your story, Holmes. Found the jewels yesterday at three o'clock in the lake, tied up in a chamois bag, didn't you? But what were you doing out in an open boat in the downpour that lasted all yesterday afternoon?"

"It was because of that downpour that I sallied forth," explained Holmes confidently. "Perfect fishing weather, so I jumped into my boat and went across the lake for some minnows. I had rowed back to within a few yards of shore when I just happened to notice the bag lying on the bottom of the lake, so I landed, tipped my boat over to keep the rain out, and waded in. Curious, you know. The water at that point was over my waist and cold, but when I opened the bag—my courage and curiosity were rewarded."

"On which side of the dock did you find it?" asked Fordney.

Holmes pointed to a spot on the sandy bottom at the left.

"Think I'll talk with the minnow man," declared the Professor as he got into Holmes's boat. He rowed furiously for about fifty yards, suddenly dropped the oars and, after glancing from the crystal-clear water to the bottom of the boat, emitted a victorious chuckle.

"Stupid of me not to have thought of that before," he mused. "Wonder if Holmes is a better fisherman than he is a liar?"

◎ ◎ ◎

Clever fellow, Holmes. Did his story fool you?

(solution on page 165)

The Unlucky Elephant

"**D**ead! Bullet hole to the right temple," said Sergeant Reynolds, as he knelt by a man lying face down, a revolver clutched in his right hand.

"All right," replied Inspector Kelley. "Let's have a look around. Dressed for the street, eh?" While speaking, Kelley picked up from the floor several fragments of glass and a right-hand glove, turned inside-out.

"Look at this glove, Reynolds. What do you make of it? And I wonder if that soiled handkerchief on the table belongs to him?"

"Gee, Chief," said Reynolds, as he turned the body over and unbuttoned the topcoat, "this is young Holman, the millionaire."

The body was immaculately clothed in the finest custom tailoring.

"Broke his watch, too. Stopped at eight-ten," continued the Sergeant, as he removed the timepiece from the vest pocket. "Let's see if those pieces you've got are part of the crystal. Yep! And look at this jade elephant at the end of the chain.

"Bumped himself off, all right, Inspector, but I don't get that glove business, or that dirty handkerchief either."

"We'd better look round and find that other glove," said Kelley.

A thorough search failed to disclose it, and while the Inspector was confident it was suicide, he decided to get Professor Fordney's opinion, because of the prominence of young Holman. After explaining the situation to the Professor over the telephone, he was puzzled by his reply:

"I'll be right around, Inspector. From what you've told me, it sounds like murder."

⊙ ⊙ ⊙

What justified the Professor's belief that
it was probably murder?

(solution on page 166)

The Professor Listens

"**W**hy the rush to get back to New York?" inquired Fordney, a few minutes after Delavin stepped from the plane. "Thought you intended spending the summer in Cuba."

"Well, if you must know, my bank failed, and I came back to straighten out my affairs."

"That's too bad, Delavin. How did you hear about it?"

He handed Fordney a clipping from the *Jacksonville Herald*:

New York, July 5. (AP)—Foundation Bank & Trust Co., one of New York's oldest banking establishments, closed its doors today...

"Sure you didn't come back to help your pal Ryan?" asked the Professor. "He's been in jail for two days. Ever since the Fourth-of-July bombing. Had a letter on him signed by you asking him to get in touch with a C. J. Wallace.

"We traced Wallace and discovered he is with an ammunition company. When the District Attorney heard you were on your way here, he asked me to meet you. He thinks you know something about the bombing."

"In jail, huh? I didn't know there had been a bombing. Wallace is a cousin of mine."

"Where did you catch your plane?"

"Why—er—Jacksonville, Florida. You see, I was staying at a rather remote place and no planes serve that part of Cuba. Really had no thought of leaving until I read of the bank failure."

"Well, you had better think of a more convincing alibi, before the District Attorney questions you."

◦ ◦ ◦

What do you think of Delavin's actions? Suspicious? Why?

(solution on page 166)

Ten-Fifteen

Professor Fordney glanced at his desk clock as he picked up the receiver—ten-fifteen.

"Hello!" came the agitated voice at the other end. "This is Waters. Could you come over right away? Something's just happened that I'd like to discuss with you. I'd appreciate it."

"Well," returned the Professor, again glancing dubiously at the clock, "if it's important, I'll be round in a bit. Goodbye."

Twenty minutes later, he was met at the door by Waters's secretary who was almost incoherent in his astonishment.

"He's dead, Professor. Dead—there in the library!"

Fordney hurried to the room and found Waters slumped over his desk with his throat cut.

"Well, tell me what happened," he said to the secretary, as he noted the position of the body, the open window, and the cigar-ash on the rug about six feet from Waters's chair.

"I came in about an hour ago, Professor, and went right upstairs to do some work. Twenty-five minutes ago, I came down and heard him talking to you as I passed the library on my way to the pantry for a sandwich. I was there about twenty minutes,

I imagine, and, as I came back through the hall, I happened to look in here, and there he was. I can't imagine who did it or how it happened," he concluded.

"Have a cigar," offered Fordney.

"Thanks, I will, Professor. It'll kind of steady the nerves."

"And now," said Fordney, "suppose you tell me the real truth of this affair."

❂ ❂ ❂

Why did he doubt Waters?

(solution on page 166)

Rapid, Transit

"I was beatin' along the Boston Post Road, about fifty miles an hour, when I looks around and sees this guy standing on the bumper fumbling with the lock on the doors. I stopped as fast as I could, jumped out, and ran round to the back. The guy had hopped off with an armful of furs and climbed into a car that was following. His partner even took a shot at me," said Sullivan, whom Professor Fordney was questioning.

"He must have been a very good judge. He took only the best you carried," commented Fordney.

"Yeah. Guess he was. Fur-stealin' is a big racket these days."

"Why didn't you report it at the next town instead of waiting until you got back to the office?"

"Well, I thought the boss wouldn't want it to get out that the furs of his wealthy customers had been pinched. He's awful particular about us usin' our heads."

"Where was your helper?"

"Just after I started out, he said he was feelin' sick, so I told him to go on home."

"Fifty miles an hour is excessive speed for that truck, isn't it?" asked Fordney, examining the all-steel doors of the massive, dust-proof moving truck.

"She's big, but she'll do even better than that!"

"Always wear those gloves when you're working?"

"Always."

"I thought so," retorted Fordney, continuing his close examination of the doors.

"Come on, Sullivan, take me for a ride in that truck. I know you're lying."

❂ ❂ ❂

How did the Professor know?

(solution on page 167)

The Professor Is Disappointed

"What'll I do, Professor?" implored Vi Cargo, as Fordney examined the ground beneath her bedroom window. Seven a.m. A fine time to start looking for a thief! Why couldn't women be more careful of their jewelry!

"I was restless all night," said Vi, as Fordney knelt beside a deep impression of a man's right shoe.

"By Jove, I thought we'd found one of your stones," he said, pointing to a leaf in the footprint. "Look at the sunlight glistening on those raindrops!"

"It was the shower that awakened me around six," chattered Vi. "It only lasted about fifteen minutes. I dozed off again and awakened with a start just as a man jumped to the ground, from my bedroom window."

"Was that just before you came for me?"

"Yes."

"Are you alone, Vi?"

"Yes. The servants are in the country."

"Then why did you have all your jewels in the house?"

"I had worn them to Mrs. De Forest's party."

"Do you know anyone who smokes this brand?" asked Fordney, picking up from the ground an unsmoked cigarette of English manufacture.

"Yes. Mr. Nelson, who brought me home last night. However, I threw that one there."

"The thief pried open this window directly under your bedroom."

"I wondered how he got in! The doors were all locked."

"Come, my dear! Don't you think you've treated the old Professor rather shabbily? I know your jewels are heavily insured and I also know of your bridge debts. Who helped you fake this robbery? Nelson?"

o o o

Where is the clue?

(solution on page 167)

A Dramatic Triumph

A clock softly chimed eight-forty-five as Professor Fordney and Halloway, dramatic critic of the *Times*, finished their after-dinner coffee. They strolled leisurely to the corner and reached the Belmont just in time for the curtain.

As the first act ended, Fordney remarked enthusiastically: "Halloway, it's magnificent! Boswell is certainly our finest dramatic actor. How he held that audience, for forty-five minutes, from the moment the curtain arose! That's genius!"

The final curtain found him even more enthusiastic in his praise of Boswell's acting.

Learning next morning of the actor's murder, he became personally interested. Sibyl Mortimer had been questioned by the police and quickly dismissed. Her alibi appeared sound. She had an engagement with Boswell last evening, but said he telephoned her shortly after nine breaking it, so the police concerned themselves with his reason for doing so.

A taxi driver, who drove Boswell and another man from the theater, dropped them at Fifth Avenue and Sixty-Fifth Street at midnight. His description of the man checked with that of Jenks,

Boswell's manager, who was missing. It was learned that his reason for breaking the engagement with Sibyl was to discuss a new contract with Jenks, about which there had been considerable disagreement.

A charred piece of the contract was found in the actor's fireplace, in front of which he lay. Jenks's cane and a vanity case monogrammed "S. M." were also found in the room.

Acquainted with the facts by Sergeant Reynolds, Fordney replied, "I'm afraid you've overlooked a valuable clue."

0 0 0

What was it?

(solution on page 167)

Murder at the Lake

"Here's all we've been able to learn, Professor. I wish you'd see what you can make of it," said Sheriff Darrow.

"Garden's cottage fronts the lake at a point about halfway between the head and foot of its mile length.

"A strong east wind off the lake that morning caused him and his two guests to abandon their proposed fishing trip. Garden remained behind while Rice and Johnson set off hiking in opposite directions.

"Rice said that fifteen minutes later, as he was retrieving his hat which had blown into the lake, he heard a shot and hurried to the cottage. There he found Johnson with blood on his hands bending over Garden, who had been shot through the heart.

"Johnson said he had gone only about two hundred yards when he heard the shot and rushed back. He claims he got the blood on his hands when ascertaining if Garden was alive. He also admits moving some furniture, although cautioned against it by Rice.

"Fortunately for Rice, we found his hat still wet, but discovered he had changed his shirt before the arrival of the police. He had also gone through Garden's desk, but said he removed nothing.

"Both men entered through the back door, though the front entrance was more convenient.

"We haven't found a gun or any other weapon and we haven't been able to establish a motive yet," concluded Darrow. "What do you make of it?"

"It's a bit muddled, Sheriff," replied Fordney, "but I would question _____ further."

❍ ❍ ❍

Of whom was he definitely suspicious—and why?

(solution on page 168)

The Professor Studies a Coat

"They covered us with a gun, and when the cashier tried to give an alarm, they shot him. Then they handcuffed me, grabbed five stacks of bills, and beat it."

"Calm yourself," ordered Fordney, "and tell me who 'they' are."

"Two fellows who robbed the bank just now," explained the excited narrator, who had rushed into Fordney's cottage at Lakeview. "I knew you were vacationing in the village, so, as soon as they escaped in their car, I ran over here."

"Didn't you call a doctor for the cashier?"

"Too late. He must have died instantly."

"How do you know the bandits escaped in a car?"

"I saw them from the window."

"Were you and the cashier alone at the time of the shooting?"

"Yes. I had just made a deposit. I guess they got my money, too."

Fordney walked over and picked up the overcoat his visitor had removed upon entering the living room.

"You seem to have had a little accident. How did you get this?" he asked, examining a long tear in the front of the coat.

"Why—I guess I tore it on the door when I rushed out of the bank. I broke a button, too, you'll notice."

"Let's see your hat!" demanded Fordney, eyeing his visitor sharply.

"Why—where is it? I—must have left it in the bank!"

"Well—let's go. The police will be interested in your story—and bring that coat with you!"

○ ○ ○

Why did Fordney suspect this man
of complicity in the holdup?

(solution on page 168)

Too Late

"**P**erhaps you'd better tell me exactly what happened," said Professor Fordney kindly to the agitated man.

"Well," continued Palmer, "Frank has been despondent and talked of suicide for some time. I thought exercise and the open air would do him good, so I suggested a vacation at my place in the country.

"We'd been there three days, and he seemed in much better spirits. Then, Thursday morning, after we'd been fishing an hour or so, he said he thought he'd try another stream about a mile away. I was having good luck, so I told him to go ahead and I'd meet him at the cabin later.

"About eleven o'clock, when I'd caught my limit, I started back. As I neared the cabin, I seemed to have a premonition of trouble, and ran the last few yards. When I opened the door, God! I'll never forget it! I'd got there not more than five minutes behind him, and yet there he lay—dead! That hideous look on his face! It haunts me! Why couldn't I have been just a few minutes earlier?

"A whiskey bottle on the table and the glass which smelled of cyanide told me the story. He'd done it, after all! I'll never forgive myself," Palmer concluded with a sob.

"Had you any visitors while at camp?" asked Fordney.

"No, we hadn't seen anyone for two days."

"Did your friend smoke?"

"Not at all."

"Was the door open or closed when you arrived?"

"Why, closed."

"And the windows?"

"Closed, too, Professor."

"If you're innocent, Palmer, why are you lying?" demanded Fordney.

○ ○ ○

What was the lie?

(solution on page 168)

Sergeant Reynolds's Theory

"**I**nspector Kelley picks out such nice messy jobs for me."

Professor Fordney smiled as Reynolds made a wry face.

"We found him lying against a boulder about ten feet from the bottom of a fifty-foot embankment of solid rock. While there were no traces of the path of his fall, the concrete road directly above him was stained with blood. I don't know why people insist on walking along the highway.

"That's such a bad curve right there. I don't suppose we'll ever find out who struck him. And then, it's possible for someone to have hit him without knowing it. And I believe that the car that did it stopped and the driver seeing how badly he was hurt, in fear, drove on."

"What makes you think that, Reynolds?"

"There are tracks of a car skidding along the shoulder of the road, and footprints in the blood where the fellow dropped on the pavement. I suppose the poor old man regained consciousness, staggered to his feet, and rolled down the embankment. That finished him. Ugh—it was a messy affair!"

"Who is he?"

"We're not sure. The only identification was a small scrap of paper in his pocket with the name Tabor. By a strange coincidence, there was a large T deeply cut in the bloodstained boulder that stopped his fall."

"No doubt, Sergeant, the murderers intended you would assess it this way, but don't you see t____ w__ n_ b____ b_____ t__ r___ a__ t__ b_____?"

o o o

What did the Professor tell Reynolds?

(solution on page 169)

Daylight Robbery

"I went to the office Thursday to do some work," Shaeffer related.

"About noon, I happened to look out the window and notice a black sedan draw up and two tough-looking fellows get out. They looked suspicious to me, and, as I wasn't armed, I hastily slammed the safe door closed and ran into the washroom—not a bit too soon, either. In just a few seconds they came in, one carrying a sawed-off shotgun. I could see them clearly.

"They looked around for a moment and one said, 'If anybody comes in here before we're through, give it to him.'

"He then went over to the safe and, after working on it for about five minutes, had it open and took the money. They certainly had a lot of nerve. Even stopped to count it! Then they leisurely strolled out the door. I called Headquarters immediately."

"How much did they get?" questioned Inspector Kelley.

"Over fifteen thousand. We hadn't banked the money from the day before because Thursday was a holiday."

"Get the license plate?"

"No. When it drove up to the office, I didn't see a license plate on the front, and I couldn't see the back. When I finished telephoning for the police, it had gone."

"Was there anyone at the office besides you?"

"I was alone. A man telephoned an hour before, however, and asked if we were open. I told him no, but I'd be there until about two-thirty. He hung up without answering."

○ ○ ○

Why did Inspector Kelley immediately arrest Shaeffer?

(solution on page 169)

A Simple Solution

The sun streamed cheerfully through the window, bringing into lively display the soft tones of the luxurious furnishings. The two houseguests, Professor Fordney and Inspector Kelley, entered the oil magnate's bedroom.

"Nothing in here to get excited about," said Kelley.

Fordney, opening the window and seeing Smith lying on the ground three stories below it, cried, "Run downstairs, Inspector. Quick! There he is!"

Kelley nodded, and was on his way. As he hurried out the door, he came face-to-face with the butler. Fordney eyed the servant suspiciously as he entered.

"When did you see Mr. Smith last?" he asked.

"About an hour ago. He had a telephone call that seemed to upset him and he came right up here to his room."

"Who brought this up?" Fordney asked, fingering an unopened letter with an illegible postmark.

"He brought it up himself, sir, saying he was not to be disturbed."

"Anyone been here since?"

Kelley's noisy entrance interrupted the butler's "No, sir."

"Smith broke his neck. I found this on him," he remarked, handing the Professor a note.

Ill health and financial trouble have made life a burden. I'm leaving my bedroom for the last time. A three-story drop and my misery will be over.

Smith

"His suicide will be a blow to the oil industry," Kelley mused, as Fordney sat down at the desk and began to write with Smith's fountain pen.

"His *death* will be, Inspector," said Fordney. "Better get the servants together. This is murder—not suicide!"

❍ ❍ ❍

What reason did Fordney have for making such a statement?

(solution on page 169)

Who?

"I was trying to stop the flow with this, Professor," said Weeds, the butler, indicating a blood-covered towel he said he had just removed from the bed, "when Jones struck at me and I dropped it."

"And I'm sorry I missed!" angrily exclaimed Jones, the chauffeur.

"Never mind that," said Inspector Kelley.

"Did you find her, Weeds?" asked Professor Fordney.

"Yes, sir."

"She's a good-looking girl," remarked Kelley, looking at the maid lying on the floor at the side of the bed. Her right hand outstretched, the wrist deeply cut, rested in a pool of blood on the polished floor. "Must have slipped off the bed."

"I don't think so. The spread hasn't a wrinkle in it," said Fordney, noting the immaculate coverlet of pink lace, the edge caught under the girl's body.

"She was almost gone when I found her," offered Weeds, "and she died before I could get a doctor."

"Is this yours, Jones?" inquired Fordney, picking up a sharp knife hidden by the girl's dress.

"Yes. She wanted it to cut the stems of the flowers I had brought up."

"I didn't see that knife when I tried to help her," said Weeds.

"Course you didn't! You put it there!" shouted Jones angrily.

"How do you know? You weren't here. And what's more, I heard you threaten her last night. You don't see any flowers here, do you, Inspector?" quietly asked Weeds.

"You're right," said Kelley. After whispering to Fordney, he continued, "Come on, *you're* under arrest. And *you*, we'll question you later!"

○ ○ ○

Whom did Kelley arrest—and why?

(solution on page 170)

Murder in the Swamp

"We'd better walk along the edge," said Professor Fordney, as they started down the only path leading through the swamp.

"I never thought of that. I was on the porch when Barton left," said Bob, as he trudged along.

"Ten minutes later, I heard a shot. I ran down the path and found him about five hundred yards from the house, bleeding terribly from a wound in the head. I dashed back for the first-aid kit and bandaged him as best I could. He died shortly afterward. Then I returned and telephoned you."

When he reached the body of Barton, he explained, "I turned him over so that I could dress his head."

"He must have been shot from over there, because those two sets of footprints are yours and the other one Barton's," said Fordney, after a careful examination. "Let's look in that underbrush."

Walking into it a few yards, he said, "Here's where the murderer stood, all right. See those powder marks on the leaves?"

While removing the branch, Fordney cut his finger.

"Better sterilize that, Professor."

Back at the cottage, as he was about to pick up an antiseptic bottle from the kit Bob had used, he observed a spot of blood on the label. Walking over to the sink, he saw Bob in the mirror above it, furtively slip a pair of scissors into the kit.

Turning slowly around, he said, "I'll have to hold you on suspicion of murder."

○ ○ ○

Why?

(solution on page 170)

Death by Drowning

"We were just getting into our boat," said the elder Carroll brother, "when we happened to notice Ridge out there in the middle of the water, just downriver of Wolf's old abandoned dock, acting very oddly. He jumped up and down in the boat, and then, all of a sudden, grabbed an oar, threw it up in the air, and jumped in.

"We rowed to the spot, and I dove in after him while my brother secured his boat. The current's fast there, but I'm a strong swimmer. I swam around while my brother rowed about, but we could find no trace of him," he concluded.

"We found the oar all right, in the weeds at Wolf's dock," interjected Riley, of the River Patrol.

"How wide is the river at that point?" asked Professor Fordney.

"About half a mile," said Carroll.

"Pretty lonely, too, isn't it?"

"It is that," replied Riley.

"The coroner's report says Ridge had received a blow of some kind on the chin. Know anything about it, Carroll?" inquired Fordney.

"No, I don't. Might have hit a rock or the side of the boat when he went over."

"How far were you from Ridge?"

"About three hundred yards, on the west side."

"Did you and your brother have on bathing suits at the time?"

"I did, but my brother didn't."

"Are there any bloodstains in Ridge's boat, Riley?"

"Well, there are stains all right, and they look like blood to me."

"I'm not surprised. Hold them both."

❂ ❂ ❂

Why was the Professor suspicious
of the Carroll brothers?

(solution on page 170)

Tragedy at the Convention

The Convention was in an uproar this morning! The Drys were making a determined stand and showing some unexpected last-minute strength. The Wets were shouting, clamoring, and stamping. The Chairman was vainly trying to restore order amid a scene of wild confusion.

As the furor reached its pitch, Hurlenson, a powerful leader of the Wets, told a companion seated next to him that he may as well have a heart attack coming on from all the excitement, and was going back to the hotel.

An hour later, the Convention was stunned to learn he had committed suicide in his room.

Professor Fordney, a guest at the Convention, went immediately to the hotel.

In Hurlenson's room he found the police, the doctor, and Pollert, an influential delegate, who had discovered him.

"The last time I saw Hurlenson was at the party last night, and he seemed in excellent spirits," said Pollert. "I arose late this morning—my room's down at the other end of the corridor—and I was just leaving for the Convention Hall when I heard a shot. I dashed directly here, but it was too late. He must have died immediately."

"He did," said the doctor. "He apparently stood in front of the mirror, took aim, and blew out his brains. There are powder burns all around the wound."

Learning that none of the maids or any of the other guests were on the floor at the time, Fordney advised the police to hold Pollert on suspicion of murder.

�𝇉 �𝇉 �𝇉

Why?

(solution on page 171)

A Murderer's Mistake

"Look, Professor! That's how the murderer got in, all right," said Tracy.

As Fordney walked over to the ladder standing two feet from the back of the house, he knelt down and carefully studied the heavy footprints around it.

"Whose room is that?" he inquired, pointing to a second-story window against which the top of the thirty-foot ladder rested.

"That's Uncle's study," replied Tracy.

Going into the house, Fordney first questioned Withers, who had discovered the body of Lane, Tracy's uncle.

"I was reading in my room," he said. "About two o'clock I heard a noise, so I armed myself and crept out into the hall. Then I heard it again, apparently in the study, so I stole down the corridor, opened the door, and rushed in. I turned on the lights, ran over to the open window, looked out, and saw a man scurry down the ladder, jump off, and run. I fired twice, but evidently missed him," he concluded.

"Were you home all evening, Mr. Tracy?"

"No. I had just put up the car when I heard the shots and saw a figure dash around the house."

"I'll take a look at your car later, Tracy.

"Withers, show me exactly how you found Lane before you lifted him to the sofa."

As Withers righted an overturned chair, fitted its legs carefully to four impressions in the rug at the right of a smoking stand, sat down, and slumped over to the left, Fordney said, "That's enough. Which one of you killed him?"

◎ ◎ ◎

Why did Fordney make this startling accusation?

(solution on page 171)

Babe Comes Through

"**S**trike two!" shouted Umpire Starlen.

"Kill the Umpire! You big bum! Thief!"

Professor Fordney turned in his place directly behind the plate to look at the excited man in the next box, waving an empty pop bottle. He smiled. Couldn't blame a chap for getting excited. Starlen did seem to be calling them wrong today. That last one *was* wide!

What a ball game! Six to three in favor of Philadelphia, last half of the ninth, three on, two out, and three and two on the mighty Babe Ruth. The crowd was on its feet, yelling and stamping.

The pitcher delivered the next throw quickly. Just as Babe connected with it for a home run, a bottle hurtled through the air with terrific force and caught Starlen on the back of the head. He went down like a shot.

Pandemonium broke loose. People screamed, and a panic was threatened.

"That's him! That's him!" shouted several people, as a policeman ran down the ramp and grabbed the man who had attracted Fordney's attention.

"Tryin' to get away, are you?" bellowed the cop.

"I didn't do it! Let go of me!" he cried, as the officer dragged him to the office.

Fordney followed. "May I ask a few questions?" he inquired.

"Let's see your scorecard, young man. H'm, why didn't you record that last hit? Everything else is here."

"Why, I was running at the time. I had an engagement."

"I see," said Fordney. "Officer, you have the wrong man. He didn't do it."

o o o

How did Fordney know?

(solution on page 172)

A Soldier of Fortune

"**Y**ou'll find Walter Briggs interesting, Fordney. He's been all over the world," said Attorney Hamilton over the telephone. "He's turned up after two years, claiming his uncle's fortune. Better dine with us tonight."

"Thanks, I'll be glad to. See you at eight."

As the three men sat around the dinner table, Fordney remarked: "You're a fortunate chap, Briggs. What have you been doing in the thirty-two years you have been away from America?"

"Well, lots of things. Mr. Hamilton, no doubt, told you I went to the Congo with Father when I was three. When he died, I attended school in England. Then I traveled for a while; did a bit of tiger-shooting in Africa, killed elephants in India, and became an ivory trader, roaming the East for four or five years. I finally drifted into Russia, where I was a technical advisor to the Soviet."

"What a jolly life you've had, Briggs!"

"Not altogether, Professor. I was in Manchuria, where life was anything but jolly. It was in China I learned of my uncle's death, so I came to New York immediately."

"Are you remaining here?" asked Hamilton.

"No. Me for Paris as soon as things are settled."

After a pleasant evening, the three men parted. Reaching home, Fordney hesitated about telephoning Hamilton. After all, it *was* his duty to advise him to check Briggs's story carefully before turning over the inheritance. As for him, he was frankly skeptical!

○ ○ ○

Are you? Why?

(solution on page 172)

Number Twenty-Six

You *must* remember that, more often than otherwise, the little, seemingly inconsequential trifles, placed together, lead to the solution of crime. Never take anything for granted; examine thoroughly what appear to be the most unimportant details. Now try your wits at this one:

"I know it sounds fishy, Inspector, but I was walkin' along Sixteenth Street mindin' my business. When I gets in front of number 26 I hears a dame scream 'Help! Murder!' so I dashed up the steps to the house, pushed open the door, and rushed in. As I was halfway through the hall, a big guy steps out of a room and says, 'Ah, there, Mr. Farrell, just in time!' I asks him what's goin' on, and just then three coppers came in and takes me, this guy, and a woman, in. Neither one of them would talk to me on the way, so I don't know what it's all about."

"I'm going around myself," replied the Inspector. "I'll talk with you when I get back."

As Kelley turned the knob at number 26, the door was violently pushed open in his face. "Sorry," said Detective Bradford.

"Just going back to Headquarters. Found plenty of dope all right. Here's something you'll be interested in," showing Kelley a man's hat initialed "D.F."

"There are three packets of cocaine under the sweatband."

"This story, of course, is fictitious," said Fordney. "There's just one, small, unimportant detail that's wrong."

$\circ$ $\circ$ $\circ$

*To be a true detective, you **must learn** to detect inconsistencies quickly, however insignificant. Quickly, now! What is it?*

(solution on page 172)

The Pullman Car Murder

"Tell your story to Professor Fordney," said the superintendent, introducing the conductor.

"Well," said Jackson, "last night just after we left Albany, lower eight let out a terrifying shriek. I was standing at one end of the car, the maid, porter, and brakeman at the other end. We met at the bunk as Briggs was gasping his last breath from a knife wound in the heart. I immediately had both doors of the sleeping car guarded as well as the doors to the washrooms. Every bunk was occupied, and by this time the passengers were milling around in the aisle.

"I began to look for the missing knife used to kill Briggs. Every passenger, even the maid, brakeman, and porter—every inch of the car and all baggage—were searched, but still, we failed to find it.

"The windowsills were covered with freshly fallen snow and an examination proved that none of them had been opened.

No one had left the car and no one had entered either washroom. I knew the knife must be in the car—but where?

"Washington, our old porter, discovered the murderer's identity by scrutinizing them all.

"I know your reputation, Professor, so you will probably have little difficulty in determining how Washington located the assassin, but I'll bet you can't tell me where I found the knife."

Jackson's face fell as Fordney quickly replied, "As there was only one possible place it could have been, you found it . . .

❂ ❂ ❂

How long did it take you to discover the knife?

(solution on page 173)

Forgery

"**C**an it be possible that this has happened to me!" thought Everett Taber, as he stood in the National Bank of New York ready to deposit his fortune. Having completed his arrangements late in the day before with the bank's executives, he was the first patron of the morning. Standing alone in the bank's commodious quarters, he regretted he had no one with whom to share his happiness.

Suddenly, as he was making out his deposit slip, he decided to use his own name, Everett Mead, instead of his stepfather's name, by which he had been known most of his life. It would be a simple matter to arrange this with the officials later. As he filled out the deposit slip on the sheet pad, Everett Mead felt a new sense of poise and self-assurance take possession of him. He gazed fondly at the name which proclaimed him a wealthy man. By changing it he could completely sever former associations and start life anew. What a wonderful day it was!

The cashier, impressed with the amount of the deposit, was very obliging and wondered, as he thought of his own meager salary, how it would feel to have so much money.

"I see you are left-handed, Mr. Mead," he said, in an effort to appear interested in such an important personage.

"Yes," smilingly.

He left the bank without further conversation. Less than an hour later, his name had been forged to a check for five thousand dollars, despite the fact that no one knew he had changed his name and no one had seen him make out his deposit slip.

○ ○ ○

Professor Fordney, acquainted with the facts, knew immediately how the forgery had been accomplished. Do you?

(solution on page 173)

The Christmas Eve Tragedy

"**P**rofessor Fordney," said Sheriff Brown, of Lake Dalton, "I came to New York to ask your help in clearing up the murder of Horace Perkins at Luckley Lodge."

"Sit down and tell me about it," invited Fordney.

"The family chauffeur, returning from the station at ten o'clock on Christmas Eve, found Perkins lying in a field, five yards off the Lodge drive, with his skull bashed in."

"He telephoned me immediately and I instructed him to see that nothing was disturbed. Arriving fifteen minutes later, I personally examined the ground so no clues would be destroyed.

"The *only* footprints to be found were six of Perkins's leading from the drive to the spot where he lay. Around the body were a number of deep impressions about two inches square. It had been snowing all day until half an hour before the discovery of Perkins.

"Leading away from the body and ending at the main road, two hundred yards away, were four lines of these same impressions. They were about three and a half feet apart in length and about fourteen inches in width. In some places, however, they were badly run together.

"A stranger in our parts is quickly noted and investigation failed to reveal a recent one. There were absolutely no other clues and I could find no motive for the crime. It has me stumped, Professor," concluded Brown.

"Give me a little time," said Fordney. "Perhaps I can help. I'll call you at your hotel."

An hour later, he said over the telephone, "Sheriff, look for a man who_____." Only such a person could possibly have committed the murder."

○ ○ ○

What did Fordney say to Brown?

(solution on page 173)

A Knight of the Bath

"**Y**ou've heard me speak of my eccentric friend, Joe Leimert, haven't you, Professor?" inquired Jud. "Great character! His costly new Los Angeles penthouse is the despair of architects, but it reflects Joe, who cares little for the opinions of others. Particularly in the matter of baths is his independence reflected. While he has six of them, he is fondest of the one leading off his own room.

"It is a large all-tile bath twenty-four feet long, fifteen wide, and seven high, without a single window. He went in to bathe a few days ago, locked the door on the inside, as was his habit, and turned the cold water full on. When he went to turn it off, he found to his dismay that the mechanism controlling the drain and the taps was out of order. He couldn't let the water out and he couldn't turn the tap off. Neither could he unlock the door, and it was impossible to make himself heard. What a predicament! There he was in a locked bath with no window, couldn't open or break down the door, couldn't let the water out, or turn it off, and he had no way of attracting attention.

"Such a situation might have disturbed most people, but not Joe. He leisurely proceeded with his bath and, when finished, nonchalantly departed."

"My dear Jud," smiled the Professor, "your friend was indeed eccentric. Of course, there was only one way out for him."

◐ ◑ ◒

How is this possible?

(solution on page 174)

Murder In the First Degree

"Well, Inspector, we have your man," said Fordney as he walked into the office. "He gave us a merry chase, though.

"What a cool one this murderer is! He calmly ate his dinner while planning the crime. He didn't give the cashier a chance—just brutally shot him down in cold blood—and all for thirty dollars. I tell you, Inspector, a man doesn't need much incentive to commit murder these days. After shooting the cashier, he made a fast getaway in a waiting car.

"Fortunately, there was a policeman having dinner in the restaurant at the time, and he gave orders that nothing was to be disturbed at the table where the suspected murderer had eaten.

"There are several witnesses who will identify him, including the waitress who served him, but no jury will convict on that alone.

"While I found none of the suspect's fingerprints, personal effects, or physical traces at or on the table, I did find there a sure means of conviction. I am positive he calmly premeditated this outrage while eating his dinner."

"I hope you're right, Professor," said Inspector Kelley, "but both he and his attorney seem confident. They claim the gun was discharged accidentally."

"They'll never get away with that. The Prosecuting Attorney will be able to prove that this man deliberately planned the crime while eating his dinner. It's murder in the first degree!"

❂ ❂ ❂

How did the Professor know the crime was premeditated?

(solution on page 174)

A Rendezvous with Death

"One runs into unique conspiracies in my work," said Professor Fordney over his after-dinner coffee. "Here is the clue to that Stone case you are all interested in," he continued, passing the following newspaper advertisement:

> *WANTED. Competent private secretary. Unusual salary and opportunity for young man speaking Spanish. Culture and refinement necessary qualifications. Address KR 164.*

"I don't see how that gave you a lead. Looks innocent enough to me," remarked one of the guests.

"Well," said the Professor, "that ad furnished the strongest link in my chain of evidence. I had information that Jack Carroll was infatuated with Stone's wife. At the suggestion of his wife, Stone answered this ad and received a reply requesting him to call for a personal interview. That interview was with death!

"Mrs. Stone, when questioned, said she and her husband had not been on particularly friendly terms recently and that the last she saw of him was when he left for White Plains to see about the position.

"I called at the newspaper office and was informed that the ad had been inserted by Jonathan Gills, Pomeroy Hotel. They remembered it because Mr. Gills had telephoned asking if there were any replies to his ad. Despite the affirmative answer, they had never been called for. I found Jonathan Gills was unknown at the Pomeroy Hotel.

"I learned from Mrs. Stone that her husband had answered the ad in long-hand and that he was left-handed and a very poor penman.

"Pondering the matter, though puzzled at first, I finally hit upon the manner in which Stone had been led to his death," concluded Fordney.

◦ ◦ ◦

*How do **you** think it was done?*
(solution on page 174)

A Rum Regatta

"Here's a story that should amuse you, Jean," said Professor Fordney to his efficient and charming secretary.

He laughed heartily as he handed her a letter from his old friend, George Collins, government investigator in Florida.

Jean read the following:

An old sailor sitting on the sands of Nassau mending his fishing net was approached by three rum runners shortly after the break of dawn. They came seeking his advice in connection with a wager they had made among themselves the night before.

The three of them, having sampled too freely of the liquor they were to take the next day to Miami, had put up three thousand dollars as a prize for the owner of the last boat to reach Miami. The fact that their boss was in a hurry for the liquor had been completely forgotten.

Sobered, they realized the ridiculousness of the wager but while anxious to reach Miami as quickly as possible, they all agreed it was not to be changed. The old sailor continued weaving the cords into his net with slow deliberation. In a few minutes, calling them to his side, he whispered exactly the same advice into the ear of each.

A smile spread over his weather-beaten face and he chuckled as the three rum runners raced to the boats and started for Miami at top speed.

"It is amusing," laughed Jean, "but he forgot to say what the old sailor whispered!"

"I've never been a rum runner, but I've got the answer."

◎ ◎ ◎

*What advice did the old sailor whisper
to the rum runners?*

(solution on page 175)

Who Is the Heir?

"As the *Île de France* slipped from her bunk, Europe-bound, John Morgan, the brother of New York's largest theatrical producer, waved goodbye to his family on the dock," said Professor Fordney.

"Arriving in Paris a week later, he registered at the Hôtel Crillon. At two o'clock next morning, he called the front desk and demanded he be given another suite immediately, saying he didn't like the view from his present rooms. This, despite the fact that he had occupied—in fact, insisted upon—this suite many times in the past.

"Because of his prominence and wealth, he was accommodated at once.

"Moving on to Berlin four days later, he registered at the Hotel Adlon. The manager, anxious to please a brother of the internationally known producer, greeted him personally. He afterward remarked how worried Mr. Morgan appeared at the time.

"At two o'clock in the morning, a repetition of the Paris occurrence took place.

"From Berlin he went in turn to London, Copenhagen, Brussels, Vienna, Bucharest, and Sofia, spending exactly four days in each place. He then went to Persia. He explained to the American Consul there that he had come to Persia to sample at firsthand the celebrated wines of Shiraz, and also to continue his search for one Mirah Svari, a winemaker he had met in New York, and for whom he had sought vainly all over Europe.

"On the fourth day, he was found dead.

"Receiving news of his death, his attorney in New York, acting on previous instructions, opened his will, in which he had left his entire fortune of five million dollars to the producer.

"But, strange as it may seem, it was found John Morgan never had a brother. What a situation!"

o o o

Under the circumstances, and according to the law,
who received the high fortune?

(solution on page 175)

The Professor Stops a Blunder

At four o'clock Thursday afternoon, Louis Mundy unexpectedly received a telegram requesting him to return home immediately, as his brother John Skidder was ill.

At eight that evening, he alighted from the plane in Washington. He had not been in the city during the past two months. Hurrying to his suburban home, he found his brother greatly improved. At ten o'clock he set out on a hike through the country, returning at midnight.

These facts were all verified.

Between eleven and twelve o'clock that night, John Skidder was murdered, and the only thing missing from his house was a note for ten thousand dollars signed by Mundy.

Skidder's secretary said the note was habitually kept at the office and that she was very surprised when he took it home that evening.

Mundy declared he saw or passed no one on his hike, but under severe questioning admitted having been near Skidder's house shortly after eleven o'clock.

A thorough investigation revealed that Skidder had no known enemies and no one, other than Mundy, had the slightest reason for wishing him dead.

Mundy was consequently arrested. As he knew Skidder lived with only an old servant (who was out until after twelve that night), the police believed he had gone unobserved to the house, demanded the note, and, when refused, had murdered Skidder. No one but Mundy could possibly profit by the disappearance of the note. As it was due in ten days and he was in no position to meet it, they anticipated little difficulty in obtaining a conviction due to the strong motive and weak alibi.

Asked his opinion, Professor Fordney surprisingly said he *didn't* believe any American jury would convict Mundy.

⊙ ⊙ ⊙

He was right. Why?

(*solution on page 175*)

The Perfect Crime

Peter Johannes had one burning ambition—to commit a perfect crime. After much thinking and careful planning, he chose burglary for his experiment and a large brownstone mansion for the scene of his action.

Learning its occupants had left town, he arrayed himself in a business suit of conservative cut, flung a light topcoat over his arm, picked up a Gladstone bag, covered with foreign labels, and set out.

He had ascertained, of course, when the policeman patrolling that beat was farthest away. At such a time he drove up in his swanky sport roadster, swung jauntily to the sidewalk, skipped up the steps, and fitted a skeleton key into the lock, which yielded easily. So far so good, he thought.

Inside, he adjusted a black mask to his eyes and silk gloves to his hands: the former for a bit of local color he couldn't resist; the latter for more practical purposes. What a jolly thing this burglaring was!

He quickly filled his Gladstone with silver and other valuables. Hurrying out, he removed his gloves after closing the door.

"Done, and not a single clue left!" he said to himself.

As he was about to descend the steps, he saw out of the corner of his eye the policeman rounding the corner. Feigning disinterest, he quickly pushed the doorbell and stood there whistling.

"Hey, you!" shouted the policeman, now standing at the bottom of the steps. "What are you doing there? Those people aren't home."

"Howdy, Officer. How goes it?" said our hero blithely as he turned to greet the bluecoat. "I know they're not home; been trying to raise someone for five minutes. Annoying, too, after running out to see them. Oh, well," he continued, "I'll be going along," as he unconcernedly picked up his bag.

"You bet you will—right to the clink," bellowed the guardian of the peace. "Your story I might have believed, but . . . Come on, now, I'm taking you downtown."

○ ○ ○

Alas for the perfect crime! What caused our hero's arrest?

(solution on page 176)

The Professor Sees Through It

"Let's go in to dinner—it's twenty minutes after six, and I'm starved," said Hawkins.

"Right!" responded Professor Fordney, his train companion, "I'm hungry, too."

The two men had met only a few minutes before, as casually as travelers do, but already seemed to find each other agreeable company.

At dinner, Hawkins explained he was a conductor on another railroad and bemoaned the loss of passenger traffic. Fordney, too, decried the Depression and its effects.

When the conductor came through, Hawkins tendered a pass with a friendly remark, and Fordney, who said he had boarded the train in such a hurry he didn't have time to purchase a ticket, paid a cash fare. Neither he nor the conductor having proper change, he borrowed fourteen cents from Hawkins.

After an enjoyable dinner, they went back to the club car for a smoke and continued their chat.

"Ever been in Savannah, Mr. Hawkins?" asked Fordney.

"Why, yes. Several times. Why?"

"Oh, nothing in particular. Charming city, isn't it?"

"Yes, it is, but I like the quaintness of New Orleans better, myself."

And so they chatted through a pleasant evening until Hawkins, with a yawn, said: "Well, it's a quarter to eleven. Bedtime for me. See you in the morning. Good night, Professor. I've enjoyed knowing you."

"Good night," responded Fordney. "I'll give you the fourteen cents in the morning. Don't let the fact that I'm aware of your deception keep you awake!"

"What?" cried the amazed Hawkins.

○ ○ ○

What did Fordney mean?

(solution on page 176)

Solutions

1. A Crack Shot

It was a dark, starless, moonless night. The nearest house was five miles. An animal's eyes do not shine in the dark unless there is a light by which they can be reflected, and a man's eyes never shine under any circumstances. Therefore, Butler could not possibly have seen any eyes shining at him in the dark. It was clearly murder.

> *And thy deep eyes, amid the gloom,*
> *Shine like jewels in a shroud.*
> —HENRY WADSWORTH LONGFELLOW

2. On the Scent

It was not uncommon for bootleggers to distill moonshine in their car radiators. Mr. Collins is showing off! Not even a prohibition agent would use alcohol in an automobile radiator in or about Miami.

> *The oil and wine of merry meeting.*
> —WASHINGTON IRVING

3. Fatal Error

The Professor knew it would take a keener pair of eyes than Bronson's to see a nod in the dark. The lights had not been turned on. Remember?

> *Darkness visible.*
> —JOHN MILTON

4. The Poison Murder Case

Unless Bob Kewley had returned home after telling the Professor he was going to the theater, he could not have known the library door was locked. The fact that he did, coupled with the strong motive, naturally directed suspicion to him. He inadvertently gave himself away.

Error will slip through a crack,
while truth will stick in a doorway.
—H. W. SHAW

5. A Strange "Kidnapping"

Rolex patented self-winding wristwatches in 1931, but most standard watches of the day could not last more than 12 hours without winding. Had Johnson wound his watch immediately before 2 a.m. Friday, the time of his alleged kidnapping, it would not have been running Sunday afternoon when he recovered consciousness and said he heard it ticking.

This act is an ancient tale new told;
Being urged at a time unseasonable.
—WILLIAM SHAKESPEARE

6. A Valuable Formula

In a small room, the intruder would *unquestionably* have heard Hyde dialing Headquarters, and therefore could not have been unaware of his presence. As Hyde had obviously lied about this, Fordney was convinced he had fabricated the entire story in order to sell the formula twice.

> *Don't tell me of deception; a lie is a lie,*
> *whether it be a lie to the eye or a lie to the ear.*
> —SAMUEL JOHNSON

7. Strangled

There had been a dry, hot spell at that place for twenty-two days. Irene Greer's hair was matted with mud; therefore, she must have been attacked elsewhere.

> *The face of things appeareth not the same far off*
> *and when we see them right at hand.*
> —EURIPIDES

8. Death in the Office

Gifford could not have been shot at the time he called Fordney, as he was found with a bullet through his heart. The Professor's theory was that Gifford wanted his death to appear as murder in order to protect his heavy insurance.

> *The heart does not lie.*
> —VITTORIO ALFIERI

9. They Usually Forget Something

The note, although misspelled, poorly expressed, and written by a seemingly illiterate hand, was punctuated properly, in two places. A semicolon and a comma would not have been used had the writer been uneducated. Force of habit had betrayed him!

You write with ease to show your breeding,
But easy writing's curst hard reading.
—RICHARD BRINSLEY SHERIDAN

10. The Professor Gives a Lesson

Cardoni said he saw the kidnappers around a table as he peered through the keyhole. Yale locks do not have keyholes.

Since your eyes are so sharpe that you cannot onely looke
through a milstone, but cleane through the minde.
—JOHN LYLY

11. Upstairs and Down

The policeman ran through the hall and unlocked the kitchen door.

The doors to the porch and cellar were locked on the inside. Had the old lady committed suicide, she could not have locked the door leading to the hall from the outside. The murderer, in leaving, locked this door and forgot to remove the key. The inevitable slip!

A blockhead cannot come in, nor go away,
like a man of sense.
—JEAN DE LA BRUYÈRE

12. Class Day

The student readily recognized the absurdity of the story that the Professor had given to his class to test their quick detection of a glaring inconsistency. At this moment in time, orchestras were not conducted during the showing of a "talkie."

Wit marries ideas lying far apart,
by a sudden jerk of the understanding.
—EDWIN PERCY WHIPPLE

13. A Hot Pursuit

Smith said he *ran* after the burglar. Had he done so he could not have known the cellar window had been chiseled open. Therefore, his story was obviously faked.

A lie never lives to be old.
—SOPHOCLES

14. A Question of Identity

As Diana Lane was walking down the corridor with her back to Nora, it was impossible for the servant to know Diana was wearing her famous emerald pendant.

There is an alchemy of quiet malice by which women can
concoct a subtle poison from ordinary trifles.
—NATHANIEL HAWTHORNE

15. A Yachtsman's Alibi

As Picus said there was no breeze, the distress flag would have hung limp against the mast, and the captain could not have seen, at that distance, whether or not the flag was upside down. That's all the Professor needed to determine the falsity of his alibi. However, Picus was a poor sailor. While the International Distress Signal is a flag flown upside down, it is by custom and by regulation always flown at half-mast.

> *... And the sea charm'd into a calm so still*
> *That not a wrinkle ruffles her smooth face.*
> —JOHN DRYDEN

16. Murder at Coney Island

Jasper said he found the woman sitting *up* in the *middle* of the chariot. The motion of the merry-go-round would have made it impossible for a dead body to remain upright in the middle of the chariot.

> *Sir, you are giving a reason for it;*
> *but that will not make it right...*
> —SAMUEL JOHNSON

17. Too Clever

The murderer tried to give the impression that Dawson had died before finishing the incriminating note. Had he written it and died before completing it, he could not have put the pen back in the tray where it was found. In his effort to incriminate Lynch, the murderer had been too cautious. A costly oversight.

> *Man's caution often into danger turns,*
> *And his guard falling crushes him to death.*
> —YOUNG

18. Bloody Murder

The Professor knew it was not suicide, because Thompson's coat, which was flung *across* the room, was bloodstained. Quite impossible if he had taken his own life.

> *Blood, though it sleep a time, yet never dies.*
> —GEORGE CHAPMAN

19. Death Backstage

There were *no* fingerprints on the gun that killed Claudia Mason. She could not have shot herself in the temple and then wiped off the revolver. The murderer neglected to get her fingerprints on the gun.

> *A fool cannot be an actor, though an actor*
> *may act a fool's part.*
> —SOPHOCLES

20. An Easy Combination

It would have been impossible for Fellows to have hastily dialed a number in the *dark*. Try it!

Haste trips up its own heels, fetters and stops itself.
—SENECA

21. A Modern Knight

The fact that the bullet was found in the body and the only trace of its firing was the hole in the curtain *below* the windowsill proved conclusively the shot could not have been fired from within the room. Rocca entered at the moment his sister shot Chase from outside. Grabbing the gun from her hand, he chivalrously protected her.

But, friend, the thing is clear—speaks for itself.
—ARISTOPHANES

22. The Jewel Robbery

The butler said that, as he called for help, Dudley, a stranger, rushed in. Owings had locked up before leaving and, therefore, Dudley could not have rushed in through a locked door. The robbery was obviously framed by Stuben and Dudley.

Absurdities die of self-strangulation.
—THOMAS CHANDLER HALIBURTON

23. Before the Coroner's Inquest

Curry could not possibly have "looked up" while rowing *upstream* and seen the action he described, which took place fifty yards *behind* him.

> *The eyes of other people are the eyes that ruin us.*
> —BENJAMIN FRANKLIN

24. The Fifth Avenue Holdup

Baldwin said, "Mr. Cross tried to call my attention to it [safe] with a jerk of his thumb" at a time when Cross was unconscious. Obviously impossible. Baldwin was lying, which there was no reason for doing had he been innocent.

> *When all sins are old in us, and go upon crutches.*
> *Covetousness does but then lie in her cradle.*
> —THOMAS DECKER

25. Behind Locked Doors

Kingston thought his boldness in calling attention to his own footprints in the carpet would distract Fordney's attention from their significance. The room had been locked for three months. Of the three men, only Watkins rushed into the room within the "spotless" house; Fordney and Kingston halted at the threshold. Kingston's footprints found near the chair in which his uncle sat dead pointed directly to him as the murderer.

> *Cunning differs from wisdom*
> *As twilight from open day.*
> —SAMUEL JOHNSON

26. Lost at Sea

It would have been impossible for Mrs. Rollins to have seen a man pick up from the deck the bag of diamonds. On a dark, moonless night at sea, one literally cannot see his hand before his face.

> *The repose of darkness is deeper on the*
> *water than on the land.*
> —VICTOR HUGO

27. A Suave Gunman

Taylor said the bandit wore a silver belt buckle. This he could not have seen, for he stated: "As the robber passed through the door, he unbuttoned his coat and slipped the revolver in his back pocket." It would have been impossible for Taylor to have seen the man's belt buckle when his coat was buttoned. As this statement was false, the rest of his account was disregarded by the Professor.

> *He draweth out the thread of his verbosity*
> *Finer than the staple of his argument.*
> —WILLIAM SHAKESPEARE

28. Accidental Death

Had the man's injuries been caused only by being thrown through the windshield, there would have been no blood on the front seat of the car. His assailant had killed him, started the car, and had then hopped off the running board, hoping the wreckage would cover the murder.

> *Forethought we may have, undoubtedly, but not foresight.*
> —NAPOLEON BONAPARTE

29. Easy Money

Wilkins said he saw the burglar pick up a stack of ten- and twenty-dollar bills from the table in the center of the large library. Had he not been guilty, he could not have known what the denominations of the bills were. It would have been impossible to have determined this from the doorway. An unconscious slip on his part. If you are doubtful, just try to determine the denomination of a stack of bills on a table in the center of a large room, from the doorway.

> *For any man with half an eye,*
> *What stands before him may espy;*
> *But optics sharp it needs I ween,*
> *To see what is not to be seen.*
> —JOHN TRUMBULL

30. Robbery at High Noon

He was suspicious of John, the nephew, of course. Upon being asked where he was at the time of the robbery, he stated he was "hauling in a muskie." Unless he had guilty knowledge, he could not possibly have known at what time the robbery was committed. He fell neatly into the Professor's trap, don't you think?

> *Let guilty men remember, their black deeds*
> *Do lean on crutches made of slender reeds.*
> —JOHN WEBSTER

31. The Wrong Foot Forward

Paslovsky, the witness, who could not understand or speak enough English to make a statement to the court, yet knew *exactly* what the conductor yelled to the motorman. The Judge dismissed the suit on these unlikely grounds.

Liars are verbal forgers.
—CHATFIELD

32. Death Attends the Party

Had Dawes fallen on the table after being shot, the motion would have knocked over the "crazily balanced glasses." As the Professor found the glasses on the table, *balanced*, it was obvious Dawes had been shot, then carefully placed at the table to give the appearance of suicide. A bad slip!

There is nothing insignificant, nothing!
—SAMUEL TAYLOR COLERIDGE

33. No Way Out

The note was written with *pencil*, yet there was no pencil found in the room. Apparently the murderer wrote the note to resemble the dead man's handwriting and through force of habit put it in his pocket.

Men are men; the best sometimes forget.
—WILLIAM SHAKESPEARE

34. Midnight Murder

Day said he got the blood on his scarf when he bent over Quale's body. As blood coagulates and dries in a short time, it would have been impossible for him to have stained his scarf unless it had touched the blood of Quale shortly after his death. Therefore, Fordney knew he must have been with Quale soon after he was stabbed.

> *Murder, though it have no tongue,*
> *Will speak with most miraculous organ.*
> —WILLIAM SHAKESPEARE

35. Speakeasy Stickup

Sullivan, the bartender, said that, as he worked the combination to open the wall safe, he *heard* the holdup man *behind him*. As he was not permitted to move, he could not have known the gunman was a *big, tough-looking mug*, as he described him. As there would be no other motive in telling this impossible story, the holdup was faked.

> *Inspiring, bold John Barleycorn,*
> *What dangers thou canst make us scorn.*
> —ROBERT BURNS

36. Behind Time

The engineer said he had not seen Nelson until he was practically on top of him. That, of course, is impossible. An engineer of a train running on a straightaway would have seen him sooner.

> *You cram these words into mine ears,*
> *Against the stomach of my sense.*
> —WILLIAM SHAKESPEARE

37. A Broken Engagement

Molly said she had retired at ten, after locking her door, and had not awakened until Fordney had aroused her. Yet a few minutes after Dot had been murdered, the Professor idly "shaped the wax" of the candle on her desk. This would have been impossible had not the candle been burning within a few minutes before he entered. Her insistence that she had been asleep, together with the strong motive, convinced Fordney she was involved, as was later proved.

Love can make us fiends as well as angels.
—CHARLES KINGSLEY

38. The Holden Road Murder

Had the butler dashed in the front door as he said he did, there would have been foot-tracks in the vestibule. Remember, the Professor "splashed his way through the mud and rain, to the *door* of 27 Holden Road," and found the vestibule spotless. Therefore, Wilkins was lying, and as Cannon corroborated his story, he was also necessarily involved.

Nay, her foot speaks.
—WILLIAM SHAKESPEARE

39. Fisherman's Luck

Holmes could not have seen the bag on the bottom of the lake during a downpour. The agitation of even crystal-clear water under such conditions would have so disturbed the surface that an object on the bottom could not be seen.

A man so lucky is rarer than a white crow.
—JUVENAL

40. The Unlucky Elephant

Holman was lying face down with his topcoat buttoned and the watch secured inside his vest pocket beneath. If his watch crystal had been broken by his fall, the cracked crystal would have been contained to his coat and not strewn about the floor. This detail would have to have been staged.

For never, never wicked man was wise.
—HOMER

41. The Professor Listens

The notice of the bank failure, appearing in the *Jacksonville Herald*, was dated July 5th. This could not have reached Delavin at a remote part of Cuba, unserviced by planes, in time for him to get back to New York on the 6th. His alibi, therefore, was completely broken, as he said the newspaper clipping brought him back.

Time is the herald of truth.
—CICERO

42. Ten-Fifteen

The secretary said he heard Waters speaking to Fordney over the telephone. As Fordney's name was not mentioned during the conversation, the secretary could not have known to whom Waters was speaking. It's the little things that count—in crime detection.

Take care lest your tongue cut off your head.
—PERSIAN PROVERB

43. Rapid Transit

The driver could not possibly have seen anyone standing on the bumper of the moving truck from the front seat.

If common sense has not the brilliancy of the sun,
it has the fixity of the stars.
—FERNÁN CABALLERO

44. The Professor Is Disappointed

Fordney pointed to the raindrops glistening on a leaf in the shoe impression. According to Vi Cargo's statement, the burglar had jumped from her window after it had stopped raining.

The shameless have a brow of brass.
—HINDU PROVERB

45. A Dramatic Triumph

Sibyl Mortimer said Boswell had telephoned her shortly after nine. As he was on the stage continuously for forty-five minutes after the curtain rose, he could not have telephoned her. Obviously she had some reason for stating he did. Fordney was quick to detect the flaw in her alibi.

It is not wise to be wiser than is necessary.
—PHILIPPE QUINAULT

46. Murder at the Lake

A strong east wind blew *off* the lake; therefore, regardless of the direction in which he was walking, Rice's hat could not possibly have blown into the lake. The Professor was naturally suspicious of him when he told such a ridiculous lie.

Is't possible? Sits the wind in that corner?
—WILLIAM SHAKESPEARE

47. The Professor Studies a Coat

As the man had removed his overcoat upon entering the Professor's living room, it was perfectly patent he had not been handcuffed. He said he ran over to Fordney's immediately after the bandits left.

Truth has not such an urgent air.
—NICOLAS BOILEAU-DESPREAUX

48. Too Late

Fordney doubted Palmer's innocence because of his statement, "I'd got there not more than five minutes behind him." There was, of course, no way he could have determined when Frank had arrived at the cabin.

In general, treachery, though at first sufficiently cautious, yet in the end betrays itself.
—TITUS LIVIUS

49. Sergeant Reynolds's Theory

The Professor told Reynolds, "There was no blood between the road and the boulder." Had the man *rolled* down the embankment, there would have been some blood on the rocks along the path his body took.

How hast thou purchased this experience?
By my penny of observation.
—WILLIAM SHAKESPEARE

50. Daylight Robbery

As no safe locks unless the combination is turned, Shaeffer's story of *slamming* it closed and then the robbers working on it for five minutes was ridiculous!

He cometh unto you with a tale which holdeth children
from play, and old men from the chimney corner.
—SIR PHILIP SIDNEY

51. A Simple Solution

Had Smith committed suicide, the window through which he jumped would not have been closed as Fordney found it.

Every crime has, in the moment of its perpetration,
its own avenging angel.
—SAMUEL TAYLOR COLERIDGE

52. Who?

Kelley arrested Weeds, the butler. He said he dropped on the bed the blood-covered towel with which he was trying to arrest the flow from the maid's wrist as Jones struck at him. Yet Kelley and Fordney found the bed coverlet *immaculate*. Had Weeds done as he said, there would have been bloodstains on the bedcover.

Blood follows blood.
—DEFOE

53. Murder in the Swamp

The two sets of Bob's footprints in the path told Fordney the story. Had Bob run back to the house to retrieve the first aid kit there would have been *four* sets of his footprints. Instead, he took what he needed to cover up his crime before they left the house.

That is to be wise to see that which lies before your feet.
—TERENCE

54. Death by Drowning

Had the accident occurred as explained by Carroll, the oar of Ridge's boat could not have been found, as it was, at the dock *upriver* of the point where he jumped in. The current would have deposited it downstream. Therefore, the Professor recommended the detention of the brothers.

More water glideth by the mill, than wots the miller of.
—WILLIAM SHAKESPEARE

55. Tragedy at the Convention

Fordney suspected Pollert because of his own statements that he did not know Hurlenson had returned to the hotel. Yet, when he said he heard a shot, he ran *directly* to Hurlenson's room.

As his own room was down the corridor, he could not have known from what room the shot came, and he had no reason to assume it came from Hurlenson's room.

Politics, as a trade, finds most and leaves
nearly all dishonest.
—ABRAHAM LINCOLN

56. A Murderer's Mistake

These murderers, like many others, betrayed themselves by a simple oversight. One look at the ladder and Fordney knew no man could have climbed up or down it. The thirty-foot ladder was placed *two* feet from the house. Any person ascending or descending the ladder in such a position would have fallen backward before reaching the top or bottom.

To all facts there are laws,
The effect has its cause,
And I mount to the cause.
—LORD LYTTON

57. Babe Comes Through

There is a screen on the grandstand behind the home plate. Fordney had noticed a few seconds before, in the box next to him, the man whom the policeman had caught running down the ramp. As he could not have thrown a bottle through the screen, and, in the time at his disposal, could not have reached either side of the screen, Fordney knew he was innocent. He had noticed the man *after* two strikes and three balls had been called, and the pitcher delivered the next ball quickly.

We must have bloody noses and crack'd crowns,
God's me, my horse!
—WILLIAM SHAKESPEARE

58. A Soldier of Fortune

Hamilton knew the real Walter Briggs had gone to Africa as a child. So, when this chap said he had shot tigers in Africa, Fordney was very, very skeptical. There are no tigers in Africa. Oh, well—look it up yourself!

A traveler without observation is a bird without wings.
—MOSLIH EDDIN SAADI

59. Number Twenty-Six

The inconsistency is this: Farrell said he *pushed* open the door. Yet Bradford, *inside* the house, *pushed* the door in Kelley's face as the Inspector was entering. If Bradford *pushed* the door in Kelley's face, Farrell must have *pulled* the door to open it.

The smallest hair throws its shadow.
—JOHANN WOLFGANG VON GOETHE

60. The Pullman Car Murder

Every piece of baggage had been examined and every inch of the car inspected. All passengers, even the maid, porter, and brakeman, had been searched. The knife was still in the car. There was nothing said about the conductor being searched. The knife was found in his pocket.

> *He was in logic a great crytic,*
> *Profoundly skilled in analytic;*
> *He could distinguish and divide*
> *A hair twixt south and south-west side.*
>
> —BUTLER

61. Forgery

The forged signature was copied from the impression on the sheet pad that Mead had used.

> *Thou strong seducer, opportunity.*
>
> —JOHN DRYDEN

62. The Christmas Eve Tragedy

The Professor said to Brown, "Sheriff, look for a man in your community who is skilled or adept in the use of *stilts*. Only a man on stilts could have made the marks in the snow you described."

P.S. The Professor was right.

> *Be the first to say what is self-evident,*
> *And you are immortal.*
>
> —MARIE EBNER-ESCHENBACH

63. A Knight of the Bath

You recall that Leimert was eccentric. No mention of bath *room* was made. Leimert's bathing quarters had no ceiling, so he climbed out!

> *If anything is spoken in jest, it is not*
> *fair to turn it to earnest.*
>
> —PLAUTUS

64. Murder in the First Degree

The fact that *none* of the suspect's fingerprints were on the dishes or silver used while eating convicted him of first-degree murder. In wiping his *own* prints from the things he had handled, he destroyed *all* prints—those of the waitress, cook, etc. A damning bit of evidence that proved premeditation.

> *The weakest spot in every man is when he thinks*
> *himself to be the wisest.*
>
> —NATHANAEL EMMONS

65. A Rendezvous with Death

No one called at the *Times* for the answers to the advertisement, yet Stone received a reply to his letter of application. The ad was inserted by Carroll under the fictitious name of Jonathan Gills and answered by Stone at his wife's suggestion. She acquainted her lover, Carroll, with this fact, and he wrote Stone, arranging the meeting at which he disappeared.

> *When any great design thou dost intend,*
> *Think on the means, the manner, and the end.*
>
> —JOHN DENHAM

66. A Rum Regatta

The old sailor whispered to each, "Run the other man's boat." As the owner of the *last* boat to reach Miami was to get the money, each one raced the boat he was driving. By doing so, he hoped to beat his own boat, which was being driven by one of the others.

Lookers-on many times see more than gamesters.
—FRANCIS BACON

67. Who Is the Heir?

John Morgan's *sister*, of course!

Let us consider the reason of the case.
For nothing is law that is not reason.
—JOHN POWELL

68. The Professor Stops a Blunder

Mundy had been unexpectedly called to Washington. Skidder's secretary said the note was habitually kept at the office. Mundy, therefore, could not possibly have known of Skidder's intention of taking it home. That was exactly the weakness in the case of the police. Despite the damning circumstantial evidence, motive could not be proved unless it could be shown that Mundy knew the note would be at Skidder's house.

How little do they see what is, who frame
Their hasty judgments upon that which seems.
—ROBERT SOUTHEY

69. The Perfect Crime

Alas! Peter Johannes had forgotten to remove his mask on leaving the house!

Whoever thinks a perfect work to see,
Thinks what ne'er was, nor is, nor e'er shall be.
—ALEXANDER POPE

70. The Professor Sees Through It

When Hawkins said, "it's twenty minutes after six" and "it's a quarter to eleven," Fordney knew he was not a railroad man. No railroad worker *ever* speaks of the time in any other manner than, "it's six-twenty" and "it's ten-forty-five."

Ask the next conductor!
There is nothing more nearly permanent in human life
than a well-established custom.
—JOSEPH ANDERSON